Part 2
Digging Deeper

Moving from
Shattered to Strong

THE FOUNDATIONS OF RECOVERY

From Sexual Addiction And Intimacy Avoidance For Christians

Matt Burton
Kevin Rose
Laura Burton

Part 2
Digging Deeper

Moving from
Shattered to Strong

THE FOUNDATIONS OF RECOVERY

From Sexual Addiction
And Intimacy Avoidance
For Christians

**MATT BURTON
KEVIN ROSE
LAURA BURTON**

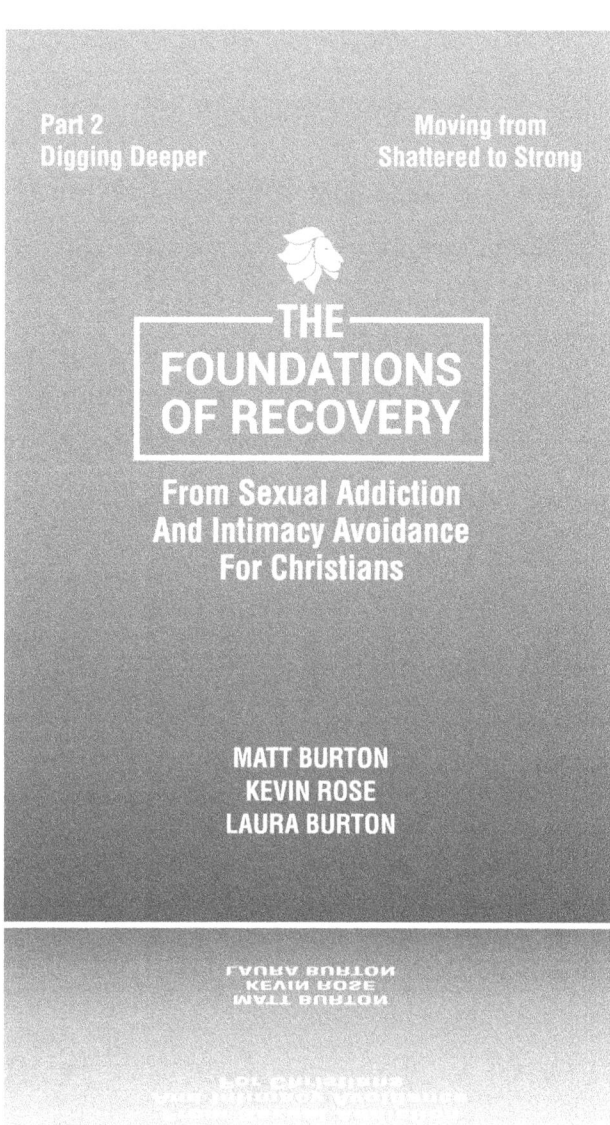

Copyright © 2025 by Becoming Well, LLC

All rights reserved. No part of this book may be reproduced or transmitted in any form, or by any means, electronic or mechanical, including photocopying, recording, or by information storage or retrieval systems, without permission in writing from the copyright owner.

The views and opinions expressed in this book are those of the author and do not necessarily reflect the official policy or position of Becoming Well, LLC

Published by Becoming Well, LLC

www.BecomingWellInstitute.com

Library of Congress Control Number

Paperback ISBN: 979-8-3493-8706-7

E-book ISBN: 979-8-3493-8707-4

Cover design by Monira

Printed in the United States of America

Table of Contents

Are You All In? 3
1. Exercise Book Completed in a Year 5
2. 3 Goals 7
3. 5 Stages of Change 9
4. Spiritual Bypassing 11
5. Wrong Thinking 13
6. Lust vs Recovery Based Decision 17
7. 1st, 2nd, 3rd, and 4th Gear 19
8. Owning It Letter 21

Lying 25
9. Lying 26
10. Outright Lying 27
11. Omitting the Truth 29
12. Gaslighting 31
13. Character Lying 33
14. Dribble Disclosure 35

Objectification 37
15. Battle Against Objectification 38
16. Pray to Humanize 39
17. Do the Opposite 41
18. Flush the Toilet 43
19. Caught Looking – Real or Perceived 45
20. Look Up 47
21. Positioning 49
22. Eye Contact 51
23. One Second 53
24. Don't Use Your Partner to Masturbate 55

Helping Your Partner Heal (Part 2) — 57
25. Wounding Agent vs Healing Agent — 58
26. Coercive Sex - Cup of Tea — 59
27. Drama Triangle — 61
28. Time Out Protocol — 63
29. Demeanor Part 2 — 65
30. The Cynical Script — 67
31. Apology Language — 68
32. Reparations — 70
33. Love Language Sandwich — 71
34. Importance of Dates — 73

Warning Signs — 75
35. SA/PA Warning Signs — 77
36. Price of Addiction — 79
37. Tips to Avoid Relapse — 81
38. IA Warning Signs — 83
39. How to Spot IA Behaviors — 85
40. Middle of the Roof — 87
41. Anger and Resentment Letter — 89
42. Releasing Anger and Resentment — 95
43. Affair Types — 98
44. Cascade Towards Betrayal — 100

Marathon of Recovery — 101
45. Self-Care Plan — 103
46. Self-Care Schedule — 105
47. Flawed and Loved — 107
48. Daily 10th Step Inventory — 109
49. The Hot Seat — 111
50. Recovery Travel Plan — 113
51. Life in Recovery — 115
52. Sponsoring Others — 117

Addendum — 121
40 ways to be IA (Intimacy Avoidant) — 129
Workgroups and Intensives — 135
Books and Courses — 143

AUTHORS' NOTE

Although the publisher and the authors have made every effort to ensure that the information in this book was correct at press time, and while this publication is designed to provide accurate information regarding the subject matter covered, the publisher and the authors assume no responsibility for errors, inaccuracies, omissions, or any other inconsistencies herein and hereby disclaim any liability to any party for any loss, damage, or disruption caused by errors or omissions, whether such errors or omissions result from negligence, accident, or any other cause.

This publication is meant as a source of valuable information for the reader. However, it is not meant as a substitute for direct expert assistance. If such a level of assistance is required, the services of a competent professional should be sought.

MATT AND LAURA BURTON
www.BecomingWellInstitute.com

INTRODUCTION

Welcome to Foundations of Recovery. Regardless of where you're at on your recovery journey, this workbook will help you chart a path of health. It will also benefit those hurt by your destructive behaviors and the ways of thinking connected to them. In short, *Foundations of Recovery* will help you get better.

This workbook was birthed out of 30-plus years of personal recovery and walking with thousands of men through their recovery journeys. Whether you are working on *Foundations of Recovery – Part 1: Ground Zero*, or *Foundations of Recovery – Part 2: Digging Deeper*, you will find that the exercises in this workbook will expand the depth of your recovery. It will also provide you with many, many tools to help you navigate and succeed in your individual and relational recovery.

Foundations of Recovery – Part 1: Ground Zero focuses on expanding your recovery toolbox, getting through the 12 steps in a year, and doing exercises around helping your partner heal, as well as maintaining a sobriety focus.

Foundations of Recovery – Part 2: Digging Deeper focuses on whether you are "all in" with regards to recovery, how to understand the destructiveness of lying and exercises to combat it, how objectification is so destructive, and how to change object thinking. It also offers a focus on helping your partner heal. You will be educated on the warning signs of potential relapse and given the tools you need to journey long-term through the marathon that is recovery.

Each workbook contains 52 exercises. We hope you will complete at least one exercise per week and finish this workbook in one year. For those wishing to accelerate their recovery, you will complete two exercises per week: one in *Foundations of Recovery – Part 1: Ground Zero*, and one in *Foundations of Recovery – Part 2: Digging Deeper*. Do this and you'll complete both workbooks in a year. Whether you get them done in one or two years, these workbooks, when done weekly and shared with your partner, will help you profoundly in your individual and relational recovery journey.

Other materials available through Becoming Well, LLC and our Becoming Well Institute here in Tucson, AZ, may be helpful in your journey. They are listed in the appendix of this book with a full list on our website. Virtual sessions for individuals and couples, Recovery Workgroups, Couples Private Intensives, Couples Group Intensives, Wounded Partner Healing Intensives, Men's Recovery Intensives, and Men's Going Deeper Healing Intensives, as well as courses, books, and videos are also available worldwide.

Please contact us for further information. You can visit our website at www.BecomingWellInstitute.com for access other resources for you and your partner

Becoming Well, LLC and Becoming Well Institute
phone number: 520-355-5322
Email address: Info@MyBecomingWell.com

Are You All In?

ARE YOU ALL IN?

Exercise Book Completed in a Year

Exercise 1

Between the two exercise books offered by The Becoming Well Institute, you will have 100 total exercises in each workbook to complete over the course of one year. Doing the math, this means 2 exercises per week. Pairing this expectation with the **Daily Times for Recovery**, you will be on track to complete them all. *Be aware that if you're in a Becoming Well Workgroup, you will have planned exercises (homework) to complete and discuss while in group 2-3 times monthly. This counts towards your expectation of 2 exercises per week.

Why do you have this expectation for yourself? Part of your growth in recovery, whether you are in a relationship or not, is creating habits of daily recovery for the rest of your life. Like your physical body, your heart and spirit need exercise to remain healthy. If you don't stay in recovery, you will drift out of health.

Think of a healthy habit you have developed in your life. How has it benefited you?

> **2 Timothy 2:15 RSV**
>
> **Do your best to present yourself to God as one approved, a workman who has no need to be ashamed, rightly handling the word of truth.**
>
> Father, there is power in consistency. I remember that it is Your approval that I need in this life. I will be diligent in reading the scriptures, recording my progress, and applying Your principles to my everyday life. Thank You for the many blessings I will reap because of this decision. In Jesus' name, Amen.

If you haven't kept up with the habit listed above, what did you begin to lose?

If you are ready to commit to this practice, this is great news! Share it with a recovery partner in a workgroup and a sponsor. I, _____(name), say _____(yes/no), I will commit to completing two exercises per week during my **Daily Times for Recovery**.

Steps 1-3 Connection: When we come together to recover, we do so with the power of accountability. Share your commitment with another person.
How does it feel to be in community with others who are also seeking health?

THE FOUNDATIONS OF RECOVERY - PART 2 DIGGING DEEPER

On a recovery call, ask someone what this commitment has produced for them. Record their answer here.

[ ]

PARTNER CONNECT Share your commitment to completing the 52 exercises with your partner. Who are you going to choose as an accountability partner to help hold you to this commitment?

3 Goals

Exercise 2

If you don't have a goal, you're not going to reach it. In individual recovery and relational recovery, it's vital to make sure that you have goals that you both write out and periodically check to make sure that you are executing them well.

That's where 3 & 3 come in:

- 3 individual recovery goals
- 3 relationship recovery goals.

These are 12-month goals. Next, you're going to write out three individual recovery goals. Make these for yourself, for your SA recovery, and for your IA recovery.

1.

2.

3.

Next, you're going to write out relationship goals. Again, do these independent of your partner. Make it come from your heart and your desires for your partnership.

1.

2.

3.

Hebrews 5: 14 AMP

But solid food is for the [spiritually] mature, whose senses are trained by practice to distinguish between what is morally good and what is evil.

Father, Your word establishes my moral boundaries. I will obey Your precepts so I can create godly boundaries in my moral life. As I practice keeping inside Your boundary lines, I will be able to distinguish other aspects of my moral life that need to be dealt with even more clearly. I will continue to hone myself in practicing what is good and holy in Your sight. In Jesus' name, Amen.

THE FOUNDATIONS OF RECOVERY - PART 2 DIGGING DEEPER

Share your relational goals with your partner. In these beginning stages of recovery, whatever their feelings may be about your goals, practice the **Empathy Exercise** regarding their feelings. Reflect here on your partner's feelings and how they are understandable in this stage of recovery.

Feeling_____ Why it's understandable:
Feeling_____ Why it's understandable:

Step 1 Connection: The powerlessness of this step is also designed to have you reflect on what is in your power. In a calendar one year from now, whether digitally in your device or on a hardcopy calendar, set a reminder to reflect on your 3 & 3.

PARTNER CONNECT Share your 3 goals with your partner.

5 Stages of Change

Exercise 3

There are 5 stages:

1. **Precontemplation**   Not yet acknowledging there is a problem that needs to change
   This is a stage where you are resistant and in denial of the seriousness of your need for recovery. Pride is at the heart of this stage.

2. **Contemplation**   Acknowledging and wanting to make a change
   This is a place of being on the fence about recovery. You may be wrestling with guilt and want change, but you may be stuck here if your actions aren't lining up with what you say you want.

3. **Preparation**   Being ready to make changes
   You have committed to change! This is accompanied by the question, "What can I do?" The heart here is humble and wanting to seek any means to the end of the destruction of SA or IA.

4. **Action**   Changing behaviors and using any tool necessary to do so
   You feel motivated here! This stage can often come and go in waves, since our willpower is not what will get us through ongoing lifelong recovery. See Step 3.

5. **Maintenance**   Frequently reflecting and revising/adding plans for ongoing change
   Reflect, Revise, and Anticipate. Once you are in maintenance, there is a responsibility to either continue to see the need for recovery or not.

Now, it is normal to go between some or all 5 of the stages in a day. Over the course of the next week, identify the stages you are in each day and describe how you could tell you were in that stage.

Day	Stages	Describe Why You Were in That Stage
1		
2		
3		
4		
5		
6		
7		

1 Corinthians 14:20 NLT

Dear brothers and sisters, don't be childish in your understanding of these things. Be innocent as babies when it comes to evil, but be mature in understanding matters of this kind.

Father, I choose to grow in the knowledge of understanding in what I need to do in order to be set free from sexual addiction/intimacy avoidance. I acknowledge my addiction, and I will use the necessary tools to overcome SA/IA. I choose to maintain my freedom from SA/IA by continued reflection, revisions, and ongoing change. In Jesus' name, Amen.

THE FOUNDATIONS OF RECOVERY - PART 2 DIGGING DEEPER

Step 1 Connection: Why are you powerless over what you are recovering from?

[   ]

PARTNER CONNECT Share the information you have learned about the 5 Stages of Change with your partner.

Spiritual Bypassing

Exercise 4

What Is Spiritual Bypassing?

Spiritual bypassing describes a tendency to use spiritual explanations to avoid complex psychological issues.
Spiritual bypassing can be defined as:

"a tendency to use spiritual ideas and practices to sidestep or avoid facing unresolved emotional issues, psychological wounds, and unfinished developmental tasks."

Spiritual bypassing is a superficial way of glossing over problems that might make us feel better in the short term, but ultimately solves nothing and just leaves the problem to linger on.
Spiritual bypassing is also often used to dismiss the very real concerns of people who are dealing with problems.

Before resorting to platitudes, ask yourself who the comment is really helping. Are you really giving someone comfort or insight, or is it just a way of dismissing a difficult situation so that you can feel better?

Causes
Spiritual bypassing acts as a form of defense mechanism. It protects us from things that seem too painful to deal with, but this protection comes at a cost. Ignoring or avoiding the issue can make stress worse in the long-term and make the problem more difficult to solve later on. While avoidance is a primary motivator behind this type of behavior, there are other factors that play a role in shaping it.

Impacts
Spiritual bypassing isn't always a bad thing. In times of severe distress, it can be a way to temporarily relieve frustration or anxiety. However, researchers suggest that it can be damaging when used as a long-term strategy to suppress problems.
Spiritual bypassing can have a few negative effects. It can affect individual well-being as well as relationships with others. Some of the potential negative consequences include:

- Anxiety
- Blind allegiance to leaders
- Codependency
- Control problems
- Disregard for personal responsibility
- Emotional confusion
- Excessive tolerance of unacceptable or inappropriate behavior
- Feelings of shame

Spiritual narcissism
Spiritual narcissism involves using spiritual practices to increase self-importance. It often involves using spirituality to build the individual up, while also wielding it as a weapon to tear others down.

THE FOUNDATIONS OF RECOVERY - PART 2 DIGGING DEEPER

Step 4 Connection: Complete an entry for your inventory

Subject	What Happened	My Reaction (Door A)	My Reason
Spiritual Bypassing *List the people, places, or groups*	*Tell the story(ies) of when you withdrawal with* <u>Spiritual Bypassing</u>	*Describe your feelings and behaviors*	*Name the nature of your reasons (ex: fear, selfishness, prideful, control, comfort...)*

Matthew 23:27 CEB How terrible it will be for you legal experts and Pharisees! Hypocrites! You are like whitewashed tombs. They look beautiful on the outside. But inside they are dead bones and all kinds of filth.

Father, give me the grace to be genuine with You and with my partner. Help me to self-evaluate and self-reflect so together, we can identify issues and make a logical and reasonable plan to resolve each issue. In Jesus' name, Amen.

Wrong Thinking

Exercise 5

Unless you become aware of false ways of thinking, you'll forever be at risk of falling back into the same traps. Changing belief systems takes diligence, but it is possible. The first step is learning to identify the **lies we believe**. The second is **replacing your wrong thinking with truth**.

- **Seeking sympathy** – you do and say things to get others to feel sorry for you
- **Victim thinking** – this allows you to avoid taking personal responsibility through powerlessness
- **Instant gratification** – this is a thinking pattern that causes you to be self-centered and to want things now. It is characterized by impatience and selfishness.
- **Blame** – this is another way of avoiding personal responsibility. It allows you to justify your behavior based on what others do.
- **Everybody's Doing It** – This pattern of thinking allows people to justify abandoning their personal commitments, morals, and beliefs because others are doing the same thing.
- **Uniqueness** – With this thinking error, you believe that the rules don't apply to you. This allows you to make yourself different from others.
- **Anger** – This thinking pattern is used to control and manipulate others. If you are confronted about a behavior that is inappropriate, outrage and anger can cause all the attention to be directed at the anger, rather than at the criticism of your behaviors or attitudes.
- **My Way** – This thinking reveals a strong desire for power. Someone using this thinking pattern resists being under the control or power of someone else. They want things to be done on their terms and under their conditions.
- **The "Good One"** – With this thinking error, your present yourself as sentimental and think of yourself as mostly good, and not someone who is in need of grace. In fact, you may even believe that God is fortunate to have you as their child because of all the good you're going to do in their world. This image of yourself as good is maintained through the good words you perceive yourself doing. This "good guy" image is, however, quickly abandoned in search for the gratification of your addiction and for excitement in general. You use sentimentality and your good works as a way to build up your opinion of yourself as a good person. Addicts will readily sacrifice others in their pursuit of sexual and other devious goals.
- **Hop-over** – this is a way of shifting a conversation to something more comfortable. By hopping over the real question, we control others, especially if they answer the question.
- **Reckless Attitude** – This pattern of thinking causes you to avoid behaviors that are seen as difficult, boring, distasteful, hard, or disagreeable. This way of thinking causes you to avoid activities where change is slow and rewards for change seem too small. Motivation and energy for responsible living is low, but energy and motivation for risky, illegal, or forbidden acts is high.

Minimizing – this is a common tendency where you believe that what you have done is really not that important. By taking one aspect of reality and minimizing it, you're able to minimize the entire act in your mind. When we minimize our actions, they seem to become unimportant, insignificant, and not really that bad. We attempt to make something big into something small.

In the table below, identify (with your partner if they're open to it) which patterns of thinking you will slip into. You will eventually slip back into wrong thinking. Your mind has been prone to think wrongly for so long. List what you think you are gaining in the **wrong thinking**. Then, list what you will gain if you change your thoughts into **correct thinking**.

THE FOUNDATIONS OF RECOVERY - PART 2 DIGGING DEEPER

Wrong Thinking	What You Think You Gain	Correct Thinking and What You'll Gain

Mark 7: 20-23 TLB

And then he added, "It is the though-life that pollutes. For from within, out of men's hearts, come evil thoughts of lust, theft, murder, adultery, wanting what belongs to others, wickedness, deceit, lewdness, envy, slander, pride, and all other folly. All these vile things come from within; they are what pollute you and make you unfit for God."

Father, I must replace wrong thinking with right thinking. I must switch out this evil belief system with Your belief system. I can't tolerate evil by convincing myself that evil is good. You are my standard and I leave behind this evil imaginary world with its wicked belief system behind. Vain imagination results in danger to myself and my partner. In Jesus' name, Amen.

ARE YOU ALL IN?

Step 10 Connection: Part of your ongoing inventory, which you have completed above, is to confess it to another person in recovery. Make a call this week. Tell someone about the wrong thinking you are recovering from. Ask them if they have been in your shoes with any of the same wrong thoughts. Then for the similarities, ask and record below what they do to correct their **wrong thinking.**

```
┌─────────────────────────────────────────────────────────────────────────┐
│                                                                         │
│                                                                         │
│                                                                         │
│                                                                         │
└─────────────────────────────────────────────────────────────────────────┘
```

PARTNER CONNECT Using your best self-reflection skills, share what you have learned about yourself through this exercise with your partner.

Lust vs Recovery Based Decision

Exercise 6

Each day we are faced with many different types of decisions. When seeking to obtain a lust hit or fix for our sexual drives, we leave breadcrumbs of many smaller decisions that lead up to those decisions. This exercise is meant to trace and uncover the crumbs you leave behind whenever you seek a lust hit. You can use the *3 Circles* exercise along with many of the other exercises in the Getting Started and Rigorous Honesty sections to help.

It comes down to identifying boundaries for yourself. Set guardrails so you can stay on the narrow path of recovery.

What do you watch? Reflect here on what types of media and entertainment you let into your eyes. Identify boundaries you need to put in place to stay out of lustful thinking.
(Examples: TV Shows, Movies, Apps on you phone…)

Who do you spend time with? This is a tough one. Identify people you spend your time with that do and don't support your walk away from sexual addiction. Whether you've told them or not, they have an influence on your life. Reflect on who is safe for you to spend time with.

Where do you go? Reflect on your commute and places you visit/vacation to. Create boundaries for where you go. This could be as simple as taking a different route to get to work.

Psalm 101: 2-4 MSG

I'm finding my way down the road of right living, but how long before you show up? I'm doing the very best I can, and I'm doing it at home, where it counts. I refuse to take a second look at corrupting people and degrading things. I reject made-in-Canaan gods, stay clear of contamination.

Father, whenever I face a decision to either lust or stay on the road to recovery, I ask for strength and grace to choose the road to recovery every time. I choose to make every decision a righteous decision by constantly identifying and observing boundaries for myself. I will not stray off the path of righteousness because I choose to be like Jesus. In Jesus' name, Amen.

Step 5 Connection: To another person in recovery, admit the decisions you plan to make to stay in recovery. Ask them and record here what decisions they have made.

PARTNER CONNECT Once you have admitted to someone in recovery your decisions regarding what you will and won't do to stay in recovery, share the same information with your partner.

1st, 2nd, 3rd, and 4th Gear

Exercise 7

Consider a manual drive vehicle. You start in neutral and shift up one gear at a time.
Let's break down your Recovery as Gears from 1-4.

1st Gear: Work on Your Recovery

SA – This involves going to meetings, staying sober, setting up boundaries whenever needed, and any other recovery tool in this book or found elsewhere that you use

IA – For intimacy growth, 80% of your work is relational between you and your partner while 20% is completing book work, doing exercises, and making recovery calls

2nd Gear: Create Safety for Your Partner

Whatever SA/Infidelity or IA recovery stage you are in, create safety with consistency over long periods of time. This is what we call your sobriety date. Until your partner feels safe, practice letting go your needs and selflessly giving what your partner needs.

Now your partner begins engaging in recovery themselves.

3rd Gear: Wounded Partners begin daily/weekly self-evaluation

Supporting your partner in this gear means opening up conversation with compassion for where they are in recovery. It is important to also keep your momentum from the 1st and 2nd gears.

*Playing the victim about how your partner is NOT in recovery themselves will never help the relationship feel safe enough for your partner. Remember that the betrayal has left them wondering if you will ever be trustworthy again, and you are responsible for the devastation caused by your behavior(s).

4th Gear: With both partners active in pursuing one another, this is what makes for a great relationship! Which gear are you currently in? Why?

Colossians 3:3-8 MSG

Your old life is dead. Your new life, which is your real life-even though invisible to spectators- is with Christ in God. He is your life. When Christ (Your real life, remember) shows up again on this earth, you'll show up, too-the real you, the glorious you. Meanwhile, be content with obscurity, like Christ. And that means killing off everything connected with that way of death: sexual promiscuity, impurity, lust, doing whatever you feel like whenever you feel like it, and grabbing whatever attracts your fancy. That's a life shaped by things and feelings instead of by God.

Father, I will always work on my recovery all the days of my life. I will always protect and create safety for my partner because Your word says to love my partner even more than I love myself. I will be a good steward of my relationship with my partner and be accountable to my partner with daily and weekly self-evaluations. I pray that partner and I pursue each other in love and friendship, because it is the spice of life and makes for a godly and great relationship! In Jesus' name, Amen.

THE FOUNDATIONS OF RECOVERY - PART 2 DIGGING DEEPER

With your partner, discuss what gear the relationship is in. Revisit what actions you can take on a day-to-day basis to help your partner feel safe in the relationship.

[ ]

Step 7 Connection: Humbly going to God and praying for aid is a practice, not perfection.

PARTNER CONNECT Be sure to discuss Part 2 of this exercise with your partner.

Owning It Letter

Exercise 8

Think about your partner's apology language. Refer to the previous exercise. Taking full responsibility with a letter is merely words on a page. What is going to matter the most when you read this letter to your partner is your demeanor. Below is an example of how you can write the introduction and body of your letter.

Introduction

To _____ (my partner),

You have devoted _____ years, _____ decades (if applicable) of your life to me.

You trusted me with your heart, to care for you emotionally, to have compassion and empathy for you. You trusted me to be faithful to you. You trusted me to make you my greatest priority, day in and day out. You trusted me to give all of me to you. You trusted me to love you, hear you, value you, care for you, protect you, validate you. I made a vow to do all these things **and I didn't.**

Body (sentence frames & examples)
I promised/committed to_____, and I didn't.

    I promised I'd see the best in you, and I didn't. I saw whatever I felt like I needed to, to justify my wrong actions.

    I promised to hear you, to value your insight, opinions, and thoughts, and I didn't. Instead, I shifted the blame to shine the light away from my selfishness.

    I promised to praise you, to build you up and share everything with you and the world because you are great, and I didn't.

    I promised I'd love you, not in the way that suited me but in the ways that you experience love, and I didn't.

I take full responsibility for_____. That's on me, that's not on you.

    I'm 100% responsible for the devastation I've caused and 100% responsible for my recovery from it. **That's not on you, that's on me. You have no responsibility in that.**

    I've played the victim in nearly every area of our relationship, rather than growing up and taking responsibility for what I've done. That's not on you, that's on me. You have no responsibility in that.

I've been_____, doing _____ to you, treating you _____. That's on me, that's not on you.

    I've been selfish, at some point making anything and everything about me. That's not on you, that's on me. You have no responsibility in that.

    You haven't been treated with the love, respect, or care that you should have. That's not on you, that's on me. You have no responsibility in that.

I showed you over and over that what I protected was myself, not you. Of course you don't feel loved by me. My actions and attitudes towards you haven't shown that. That's not on you, that's on me. You have no responsibility in that.

ARE YOU ALL IN?

_____

Step 9 Connection: You will write a section in your amends letter that is like this Owning It letter. When you are prepared, be open to asking if your partner will forgive you. Still, it is important to be open to their "no" as an answer. This is because, in their healing process from pain, they might not be ready to forgive yet. That is ok and understandable. Write how you would feel if they were ready to forgive and said, "yes I forgive you," or if they said, "no I don't/can't forgive you yet."

"yes"

"no"

Matthew 3: 8 AMP

So produce fruit that is consistent with repentance [demonstrating new behavior that proves a change of heart, and a conscious decision to turn away from sin];...

Father, as I write my Owning It letter, I ask for Your grace and wisdom to write down the correct words with humility and remorse. You saw all that I have done, and I truly am repentant of my sins and how I grieved You. I am truly remorseful for breaking my vows and grieving my partner who trusted me with all their heart. Thank You for Your loving kindness and tender mercies. I ask that through this Owning It letter, You heal my partner's mind, will, and emotions. Please heal my partner in every area that I have violated them so selfishly. In Jesus' name, Amen.

Lying

THE FOUNDATIONS OF RECOVERY - PART 2 DIGGING DEEPER

Exercise 9 — Lying

Most wounded partners tell us that, as hard as it is to forgive betrayal, it's even harder to forgive the deception surrounding the betrayal. The fact that the wounding partner had a secret life that they knew nothing about can be a hard thing to get over. It is even harder to get over when someone keeps lying. After a while, the wounded partner begins to wonder if the wounding partner is even capable of telling the truth. This can seriously affect their willingness to move forward with the relationship.

Additionally, when the wounding partner repeatedly lies, they send the message that they are more interested in protecting themselves than they are in caring for their partner's broken heart.

Trust is pivotal to all healthy relationships. The whole reason we do the work we do is to help couples rebuild the trust that has been torn down by betrayal. Lying and deception not only break trust, but they also lead to more lies and deception to cover up the initial lying and deception. This results in a never-ending downward spiral that ultimately leads to the complete breakdown of the relationship.

Lying also prevents the deep, important conversations that are at the core of committed relationships from happening because distrust can often lead to withdrawal on the wounded partner's part. A lack of communication will also lead to a breakdown of the relationship.

Outright lying, half-truths, lies by omission, character lies, and even carelessness with seemingly minor details will hamper momentum toward the recovery of the relationship. The next few exercises are dedicated to these different categories of lies.

How does lying break down and harm a relationship?

Why is lying to someone against your moral code?
Explain a time when you were guilty of lying.

> **Proverbs 12:22 MSG**
>
> **God can't stomach liars; he loves the company of those who keep their word.**
>
> Father, lying is abhorrent to You so it should also be abhorrent to me. I am alive to Christ Jesus and embrace His truth, and I am dead to sin. The sin of lying will no longer be a part of my character. I decide to walk in truth and the truth will set me free. In Jesus' name, Amen.

Step 4 Connection: At the heart of your lies, what did you think you were gaining when you lied to your partner?

PARTNER CONNECT If you have been lying to your partner, you must admit this to them. Make a recovery phone call to prepare yourself. At a calm moment, admit to your partner what you have been lying to them about. Make a recovery phone call after you have the discussion to process what was said.

Outright Lying

Exercise 10

Refer to the *Lying* exercise for definitions and explanations around the consequences of lying.

Here in this exercise, you will recall times in which you have outright lied in order to avoid intimacy or hide your sexual addiction. If you keep any of these lies hidden, betrayal is multiplied by the duration you have kept the lie to yourself. The table below is broken into the Situations you've lied about, the IA or SA Behavior behind the lie, and the Consequences of keeping each lie hidden. *Use additional paper if needed.

Outright Lie Situation	IA or SA Behavior	Consequences

> **Psalm 101: 7 ESV**
>
> **No one who practices deceit shall dwell in my house; no one who utters lies shall continue before my eyes.**
>
> Father, I do not want to be separated from You. No lie is worth losing my relationship with You. No lie is worth further torturing my spouse. My spouse should have never been exposed to my unfaithful thoughts/feelings/purposes and actions. Lying is an abomination to You. I rid myself of all lies and deceit of every kind. Give me the grace to be honest every time in every way. Thank You for answering my prayer. In Jesus' name, Amen.

Step 4 Connection: Count these entries towards your inventory. In general, know how lying has benefited you throughout your life and in general how lying has damaged your relationships.

PARTNER CONNECT With your partner, discuss what you have learned about your tendency to lie. Share with them why you think you do it. If there are things you have lied to them about, admit it to them. Make a recovery phone call to make sure you are in the right frame of mind to do this without defending or getting angry. Make a recovery phone call after you talk to your partner to help you process what was said.

Omitting the Truth

Exercise 11

Refer to the *Lying* exercise for definitions and explanations around the consequences of lying.

Here in this exercise, you will recall times in which you have lied by omission in order to avoid intimacy or hide your sexual addiction. If you keep any of these lies hidden, betrayal is multiplied by the duration you have kept the lie to yourself. The table below is broken into the Situations you've lied about, the IA or SA Behavior behind the lie, and the Consequences of keeping each lie hidden. *Use additional paper if needed.

Omission Situation	IA or SA Behavior Most Related	Relational Consequences

> **Psalm 32: 2 ESV**
>
> **Blessed is the man against whom the Lord counts no iniquity, and in whose spirit there is no deceit.**
>
> Father, I will not lie by omission. I will not lie, period. I choose to please You so You can view me as a person who has no deceit. Then my partner will view me in the same light, my prayers will be answered, and our relationship blessed beyond measure. In Jesus' name, Amen.

Step 5 Connection: On a recovery call this week, confess these situations where you have lied. Make sure to explain what the consequences are. Record the feelings you felt confessing and why.

PARTNER CONNECT If you have lied by omission to your partner, you will need to admit this to them. Prepare yourself to do this by making a recovery phone call and/or discussing it during group. Once you have prepared, tell your partner how you have lied by omission. Make a recovery phone call after you talk to your partner to help you process what was discussed.

Gaslighting

Exercise 12

This is the action of deliberately wounding a partner by:

- Questioning their reality or what they are experiencing
- Creating a prison of psychological trauma, anxiety, isolation, and depression
- Refusing to admit past gaslighting actions (a continual gaslighting)

Here are the different modes of gaslighting found in dysfunctional relationships:

- **Countering:** Questioning someone's memory of events
- **Withholding:** Pretending not to understand what someone is talking about or refusing to accept the validity of someone's experience
- **Forgetting:** Pretending to have forgotten something or denying that something happened
- **Trivializing:** Making someone's concerns or feelings seem unimportant or irrational
- **Diverting/Blocking:** Changing the subject or focusing on the credibility of what is being said instead of the content. (This can be a focus on specific facts rather than the general issue)

If you've gaslighted in your relationship, the good news is you can take responsibility today. But what does it sound like when you gaslight? Here are some examples: "You never remember things correctly."
"I never said that."
"You're being too sensitive."
"That never happened."
"I never understand what you're talking about."
"Your memory is bad. You need to see someone."
"You seem off. You need help."
"You're crazy."
"The kids think you're crazy."
"This is why you don't have any friends."
"You can never take a joke."
"You're the one gaslighting me."
What are the motives behind why you gaslight?
Discuss this with another in recovery who also has this struggle.

I gaslight by saying...

Step 6 Connection: Ask God for the removal of this defect of character. Acknowledge the pain it has caused. Praise God and choose to trust that He can help you eliminate thoughts and words that would hurt your partner.

Isaiah 55:7 NET

The wicked need to abandon their lifestyle and sinful people their plans. They should return to the Lord, and he will show mercy to them, and to their God, for he will freely forgive them.

Father, Your word says that lying and gaslighting is the native language of satan. I refuse to mimic him again! I follow after You! You are my God and I am holy and truthful like my Father in Heaven! In Jesus' name, Amen.

PARTNER CONNECT Gaslighting has hurt your partner. It has messed with their sense of reality and has made them feel crazy. If you have been gaslighting your partner, or have gaslighted them in the past, you must admit it to them. Make a recovery phone call to get your head in the right space to admit ways in which you have gaslighted your partner. In a calm moment, tell them. Make a recovery phone call after the conversation to help you process what was discussed.

Character Lying

Exercise 13

Refer to the *Lying* exercise for definitions and explanations around the consequences of lying.

Here in this exercise, you will recall times in which you have lied to protect your ego, avoid intimacy, or hide your sexual addiction. If you keep any of these lies hidden, betrayal is multiplied by the duration you have kept the lie to yourself. The table below is broken into the Situations you've lied about, the IA or SA Behavior behind the lie, and the Consequences of keeping each lie hidden. *Use additional paper if needed.

Omission Situation	IA or SA Behavior Most Related	Relational Consequences

Ephesians 4: 22,25 AMPC

Strip yourselves of your former nature [put off and discard your old unrenewed self] which characterized your previous manner of life and becomes corrupt through lusts and desires that spring from delusion; Therefore, rejecting all falsity and being done now with it, let everyone express the truth with his neighbor, for we are all parts of one body and members one of another.

Father, I will not lie under any circumstances. I will not allow any form of lie to leave my lips or insinuate a lie with my body or posture. I am a person of excellent character by choice. I choose to first please You, Lord, with all of my heart and I choose to please my partner. I am a trustworthy person and I walk in a way that is honorable. In Jesus' name, Amen.

Step 6 Connection: Pride is at the heart of a character lie. Write a prayer expressing an open heart to transformation. Sit with the humility of the pain your pride has caused. Then humbly ask God to help remove the pride that has driven you to inflate your ego.

PARTNER CONNECT Using your best self-reflection skills, share what you have learned about yourself with your partner.

LYING

Dribble Disclosure

Exercise 14

This terminology, dribble disclosure, is used to describe truth that is revealed slowly over time. What motivates someone who has wronged their partner is fear. Fear has driven you towards hiding the truth because you think that you are protecting the relationship.

Is this true about your story? Have you withheld the full truth in fear of losing your partner, or with a misconception of not wanting to cause them pain? Answer these questions and express your motivations to withhold the full truth.

[ ]

Research has shown that the deception over a long period of time is harder to get over than the infidelity itself. This is because the path towards rebuilding trust is marked with honesty. When that honesty is tarnished over time by continued deception, rebuilding trust is exponentially more difficult.

Through the view of your partner, why would it be difficult for them to trust you if you dribbled your disclosure?

[ ]

The hope you can have is that, once you have been fully honest, then and only then can you look forward to your partner, in time, participating in building a loving relationship through trust and commitment. Before that day of full honesty and transparency, your partner will wonder if the truth is all there. A polygraph can be helpful here to a) show your partner your willingness to prove, to the highest measure, your full honesty and disclosure of infidelity and b) provide enough safety for your partner to consider engaging in building trust in the relationship.

Step 7 Connection: By humbly asking God to remove your character defect of lying, you are opening yourself up to the possibility of living a more full and intimate life. Describe the feeling you and your partner would have if rigorous honesty became a norm in the relationship, and if both of you felt safe to do so.

[ ]

> **Luke 8:17 NASB For nothing is concealed that will not become evident, nor anything hidden that will not be known and come to light.**
>
> Father, grace me with empathy towards my broken partner. Help me to own up to what I have done. Help me to reveal all that I have done to break the covenant with my partner in a manner that is complete and with as little pain as possible. In Jesus' name, Amen.

Objectification

THE FOUNDATIONS OF RECOVERY - PART 2 DIGGING DEEPER

 Exercise 15　　Battle Against Objectification

This is an exercise specific to the problem of lust and the objectification of anything or anyone that is the subject of our sexual addiction. This is the battle of the heart. Many times, addicts will express that they can't help thinking sexual thoughts. This is due in part to a psychological freeway of pleasure associated with modes of "acting out" such as fantasy and pornography. To turn off the freeway, we must pave a new road, humanizing the person of our lustful temptation.

Objectification can happen at any given moment. While driving, watching TV, at work, or even towards our partner, we diminish someone to a body part to be used in our sexual addiction. Yes, looking at our partners, lovers, or spouses as an object of sexual pleasure leaves no room for treating them as humans.

Name the places/areas in which objectification occurs.

[ ]

Next, we battle objectification by humanizing the people. List human character traits or identities of the people you objectify. (Ex: mother, daughter, _____(career), sister, child of God, _____(personality trait)…)

[ ]

Write a prayer for the most recent person you objectified, highlighting their human identity. Refer to the exercise *pray to humanize* for assistance.

[ ]

Step 4 Connection: Make a list of times (in general) when you objectified for your sexual addiction. Add these general mistreatments to your inventory of sexual addiction.

[ ]

PARTNER CONNECT This exercise should not be shared with your partner, as the information here will likely cause them pain.

> **Philippians 4:8 TLB**
>
> **And now, brothers, as I close this letter, let me say one more thing: Fix your thoughts on what is true and good and right. Think about things that are pure and lovely, and dwell on the fine, good things in others. Think about all you can praise God for and be glad about.**
>
> Father, I dedicate my thoughts, life, and my imagination to You. You deserve to be honored in the deepest, most intimate part of my being. I will fill my mind with Your word so it permeates my thoughts and imagination. Filling myself with Your word and filling my mind and heart with Your praises eliminates room for sinful thoughts to exist. I choose to fill the real estate of my mind with Your word and Your wisdom. In Jesus' name, Amen.

OBJECTIFICATION

Pray to Humanize

Exercise 16

Pray to Humanize

When our mind wanders, whether into lust, fantasy, or *negative narrative*, we can choose in that moment to snap our *rubber band* and pray for our partner or the subject of our lust. The point is, we cannot objectify, lust over, or think negatively about someone and pray for them at the same time. Fill in the blanks of this prayer for anything that satisfies the above categories:

"God, I surrender my right to_____ (lust, objectify, think negatively about…).

I pray for them as_____ (someone's daughter, wife or future wife, sister…).

I pray for their_____ (well-being, career, growth into healthy people…).

And I ask for you to show me what I need right now and who I am in you."

Now, rewrite the prayer for yourself two ways, a) for sex addiction and b) for *negative narrative*.

a)

b)

Job 31:1, 9-12 ERV

"I made an agreement with my eyes not to look at a young woman in a way that would make me want her… If I have desired another woman or waited at my neighbor's door to sin with his wife, then let my wife serve someone else, and let other men sleep with her. To do such a thing would be shameful, a sin that must be punished. Such sin is like a fire that burns until it destroys everything. It would completely ruin my life's work."

Father, it is pure evil to desire any person who is not my spouse and I know that this is abhorrent in Your sight. I respect all people because they are made in Your image. They belong to someone else and I will never impose my will upon them in any way, shape, or form. I will pray for blessings upon them. Then I will pray for blessings over my partner and remember all of the attributes that make them so invaluable to me. I will not position myself so that my life's work is ruined. I will position myself for God's favor and a blessed relationship with my partner. In Jesus' name, Amen.

THE FOUNDATIONS OF RECOVERY - PART 2 DIGGING DEEPER

How many times a day do you pray? How will prayer help you and your recovery?

[ ]

Step 3 Connection: Prayer is a way to turn our will, passions, lusts, and desires over, surrendering our life. This is a big step. This comes with a gift of desperation for God's way, not our own. Explain your desperation for a new way to live and a new way to think about others.

[ ]

PARTNER CONNECT Take a moment to write down 3 things that you appreciate about your partner. Share these with them today.

OBJECTIFICATION

Do the Opposite

Exercise 17

Whether you're recovering from lust, sex addiction, infidelity, betrayal, or intimacy avoidant behaviors, the fact is that your life has become unmanageable. You need to change the choices and roads you used to walk on. You will need to think about the minute-by-minute, hourly, and daily choices you make. Recovery is day-to-day. Alcoholics Anonymous calls recovery "one day at a time." This is our mentality to follow the *One Path* of recovery.

You will need to think of these actions and what their opposite may be. For example:

- watch TV/MA shows vs. create an entertainment boundary
- lust over a woman jogging on the sidewalk vs. pray for her/snap your rubber band/1 second rule
- ruminate on negative thoughts about your partner vs. remind yourself of a gratitude about them
- play the victim about the patience in atonement vs. remind yourself of the responsibility you are taking

Create 10 opposites you can choose in your recovery to practice. It *is* practice. If you are struggling with thinking of more, make a call to someone in recovery and think of more to add.

Situations/Triggers/Temptations	I choose the opposite by doing…
1.	1.
2.	2.
3.	3.
4.	4.
5.	5.
6.	6.
7.	7.
8.	8.
9.	9.
10.	10.

Romans 2:5-7 CEB

You are storing up wrath for yourself because of your stubbornness and your heart that refuses to change. God's just judgment will be revealed on the day of wrath. God will repay everyone based on their works. On the one hand, he will give eternal life to those who look for glory, honor, and immortality based on their patient good works.

Father, give me the grace to train myself to do the opposite of evil. I am dead to sin, and I am alive to Christ! Instill in me a deep hatred for sin and a deeper love for You. I choose to be righteous! In Jesus' name, Amen.

THE FOUNDATIONS OF RECOVERY - PART 2 DIGGING DEEPER

Step 1 Connection: Which of the 10 above are you powerless over happening? Admit these and associate a feeling with each that you are powerless over.

[ ]

PARTNER CONNECT With your partner, share 3 of the 10 "opposite" things that you are going to do to stay in recovery. Have you identified how you are going to keep yourself accountable for doing these things? Share your ideas for accountability with your partner.

OBJECTIFICATION

Flush the Toilet

Exercise 18

This saying is commonly associated with getting rid of harmful, damaging drugs in a desperate act of "getting rid of" the tool of your self-destruction. In sexual addiction or intimacy avoidance, flushing the toilet would be a middle circle behavior *(see the 3 Circles Exercise)* that can cut off your acting out and redirect you towards health.

It's not a matter of if but *when* you will need to "flush" a sexual temptation of lust or a negative thought about your partner. The question you must ask yourself is, "Am I desperate enough to want to completely rid my life of these destructive behaviors?" Desperation for change is a gift, a posture, a recognition of guilt. Picture your toilet. It's dirty. Taking destructive thoughts and behavior, mentally throwing them into the toilet, and choosing to flush them down is a practice, not a one-time event.

If you let negative, dirty, and/or destructive thought patterns stay in your heart, what are the outcomes?

What lustful thoughts or negative narratives about your partner are you choosing to flush?

Pick a thought you would like to flush today. How does it feel to visualize it leaving your mind and going down the toilet? Reread your *appreciation & resignation letters* associated with what you flushed.

Step 6-7 Connection: Remember each of your defects of character and write a statement of flushing the toilet for each.
(Example: God, I surrender this _____(sexual temptation/negative narrative), and I flush it down the toilet)

> **Acts 3:19 AMP**
>
> **So repent [change your inner self-your old way of thinking, regret past sins] and return [to God-seek His purpose for your life], so that your sins may be wiped away [blotted out, completely erased], so that times of refreshing may come from the presence of the Lord [restoring you like a cool wind on a hot day]...**
>
> Father, I choose to get rid of damaging thoughts/behaviors/visuals/relationships, just like flushing bad drugs down the toilet. It's a done deal. My sins are gone and You will refresh me and restore me from all destruction. Thank You so very much for Your loving kindness and tender mercies towards me! In Jesus' name, Amen.

OBJECTIFICATION

Caught Looking – Real or Perceived

Exercise 19

"Our eyes betray us" is an understatement in sexual addiction recovery. Whatever the degree of sexual betrayal, when your partner suspects you were looking at an attractive woman in lust, their perception is what matters in the moment. Whether you were looking or not, their perception that you did reminded them of all the hurt associated with your sexual infidelity and betrayal. So, we *Hear and Validate* the pain they are experiencing in the moment.

- "I can tell you are in pain from _____."
- "I have hurt you in the past with ogling and lusting over other women. I am guilty of that, and I take full responsibility for that."
- Tell the Truth: "I was/wasn't looking at or lusting over that person."
- "Regardless, I have been guilty of that and I am terribly sorry for it, and it makes sense for you to feel_____."
- "What do you need from me at this moment?"

The point is, their perspective and pain must be acknowledged and met with as much empathy as you can muster. This is truly centered on humility and the surrender of defensiveness. Your ego is not what matters here, their perspective is.

Turn the tables around. Explain the pain you would feel if your partner acted out sexually with another person, and the pain you'd feel if you caught them looking at someone in lust.

Then, ask your partner to explain the feelings they'd have if they caught you looking at and lusting over another.

Matthew 5:27,28 MSG

You know the next commandment pretty well, too: Don't go to bed with another's spouse. But don't think you preserve your virtue simply by staying out of bed. Your heart can be corrupted by lust even quicker than your body. Those ogling looks you think nobody notices- they also corrupt.

Father, I choose to keep myself pure in mind and in body. I will love You with all my heart, mind, soul, and strength, and I will love my neighbor as I love myself. I know that where my mind goes, my body will follow. I will keep my mind pure so my actions and behaviors will follow my pure thoughts, intents, and purposes. I choose to be like Jesus. In Jesus' name, Amen.

THE FOUNDATIONS OF RECOVERY - PART 2 DIGGING DEEPER

ALL Step Connection: Since the steps are in the context of "we," ask someone who's been in recovery longer than you what this interaction looks like. How does it look if done in a responsible way or a destructive way in their relationship? Share what it looks like in your relationship. Record what they say here, and any similarities.

```
┌─────────────────────────────────────────────────────────────────┐
│                                                                 │
│                                                                 │
│                                                                 │
│                                                                 │
└─────────────────────────────────────────────────────────────────┘
```

PARTNER CONNECT With your partner, be sure to share what you wrote in the "Turn the Tables Around" section before moving on to other parts of the exercise.

OBJECTIFICATION

Look Up

Exercise 20

This is a practice much like many of the tools provided in this exercise book. They are not a one-time event. Looking up can keep our focus, attention, and perspective on things greater than the shame, guilt, and destruction we have caused.

So, straighten your posture, look yourself in the eyes, and get ready!

By looking others in the eyes and then tracking our attention upward, we can practice multiple exercises while maintaining fidelity for our partner. Your partner will see where your eyes point, throughout your recovery and perhaps indefinitely. It's valid that they care where your eyes go and where you are looking. By looking up and maintaining eye contact, when necessary, you can navigate away from tempting locations in the area.

When you look up you can: pray to humanize, hear and validate, battle objectification, flush the toilet, take a breath, pause, seek God's will, take a thought captive, and surrender it.

How have your eyes betrayed you, and caused destruction for your heart, your partner, and those you look at?

Proverbs 4: 25-27 MSG

Keep your eyes straight ahead; ignore all sideshow distractions. Watch your step, and the road will stretch out smooth before you. Look neither right nor left; leave evil in the dust.

Father, I consecrate my eyes and my vision to You. I will ignore all distractions and keep my focus on pleasing You in all that I do. As I please You, I know that I am also pleasing my partner and keeping the door open for Your blessings upon our relationship. In Jesus' name, Amen.

What benefits could you and the ones you love gain from your eyes being trained to look up?

Look into the mirror and explain your day to yourself. Hear and validate yourself for the feelings you had about the day, all while looking into your eyes and up. Practice this in the mirror and in the world for the next week.

Day #	1	2	3	4	5	6	7
Check Box							

Step 7 Connection: When an intrusive thought comes, pray to ask God to remove the defect, take it captive, speak a verse over the thought, and surrender your will to God – all while looking up!

Reflect on the experience in the space below.

OBJECTIFICATION

Positioning

Exercise 21

Picture yourself sitting in your favorite restaurant with your partner. The booth you usually sit at was taken, so you are given a table at which your chair is facing the hall leading in and out of the kitchen. Directly in your line of sight, you see waitstaff going in and out of the kitchen. Your partner's seat, across from you, is facing other booths. Which "position" is better for you to have sat in?

The story above happens more often than we realize. We can use positioning to our advantage when strategically avoiding temptations to ogle or gaze at women passing by our view. If we can create less traffic in our peripheral view by "positioning" ourselves in a different seat, then we do so. This helps our partners feel safe and helps us in our battle against lust. The goal is to be able to focus more on our partner and not what's going on around us. To honor the relationship with our eyes.

It may be good to check your positioning at a restaurant, at work, while walking through a store, in a supermarket line, or at the beach. Think about how positioning would help you in the battle against lust.

Name the situations in which your eyes wander, and lust is a temptation. Think about daily events. Think about special events. Think about the locations that always seem to present a challenge for you.

> **1 Corinthians 10: 12, 13 CEV**
>
> **Even if you think you can stand up to temptation, be careful not to fall. You are tempted in the same way that everyone else is tempted. But God can be trusted not to let you be tempted too much, and He will show you how to escape from your temptations.**
>
> Father, the fear of the Lord is the beginning of wisdom. It is wise to position myself in a way that will keep me pure in every situation. I position myself for success in being honorable to You and being honorable to my partner. In Jesus' name, Amen.

For each of the situations or locations above, create a plan to re-position yourself. Discuss this on a phone call with another person in recovery.

Step 4 Connection: If you haven't done so already, add the situations or locations in which you have lusted over women to your inventory. Process each within the table provided for your inventory or in a separate journal you used for inventory.

PARTNER CONNECT With your partner, share your plan for positioning and explain why this is an important part of your recovery. Explain to them that you may occasionally need to change positions when in a crowded area like a restaurant.

OBJECTIFICATION

Eye Contact

Exercise 22

Many times, years go by when your lust and objectification over the body are the first thing you notice about a person. Your mind has been preconditioned to do this from pornography and media, and reinforced by society. We need to make a conscious choice to see a person in a different way. This begins with healthy communication with your partner and those of the opposite sex in general.

If you and your partner are sexually active at the moment, giving her eye contact will help you to see her, connect in intimacy, and keep you from objectifying her as well.

Giving eye contact while in discussion keeps your eyes from wandering down. Pair this exercise with the *look up* method and *humanize by prayer* to maximize your recovery.

When you communicate with your partner, does she appreciate your eye contact? Why do you think she does?

When and where have your eyes betrayed you? Make a list of places you'll need to prepare to maintain eye contact.

Bookend a situation this week where you will need to keep eye contact with another in recovery. Describe how it felt to keep eye contact and healthy communication.

2 Timothy 2:22 TLB

Run from anything that gives you the evil thoughts that young men often have, but stay close to anything that makes you want to be right. Have faith and love, and enjoy the companionship of those who love the Lord and have pure hearts.

Father, from this day forward, I make a conscious choice to never objectify anyone again. We are Your creation and I will worship You and not the creation for it is idolatry. My eyes are only for my partner who I choose to love with all of my heart in all purity and godliness. I choose to please You in thought, feelings and purposes and I choose to be faithful to the partner that You have blessed me with. In Jesus name, Amen.

Step 6 Connection: Are you ready to have God work on your eye contact? Write a statement for why/why not.

[ ]

PARTNER CONNECT Share with your partner what you wrote about why you think they appreciate eye contact. Do they agree with what you wrote? Ask them if they have any additional input. Write down what they say.

OBJECTIFICATION

One Second

Exercise 23

The moment you notice an attraction towards someone other than your spouse, look away! This exercise is simple when it stands alone. The longer you look, the longer you are drinking lust and fueling fantasy for your sex addicted mind. Your brain will crave another look, but you will have to practice doing the opposite of what you want. This is the destructive habit of rubbernecking that many sex addicts battle with.

Pairing this exercise with others can be helpful such as *flushing the toilet, doing the opposite,* and *humanizing with prayer.* By choosing something else for your mind to focus on, you're choosing to be in recovery and to be free from the temptation of lust.

Prayer can be especially useful in an instant.

Recall the first two parts of the *Humanize by Prayer* exercise:

"God, I surrender my right to_____ (lust, objectify, think negatively about...)

I pray for them as_____ (someone's daughter, wife or future wife, sister...)."

Write these two lines of prayer in your own words.

[ ]

Name a time, place, and situation where you "looked too long" And lusted when your partner was with you.

[ ]

How will your partner benefit from you being faithful with your eyes?

[ ]

---

2 Timothy 2:22 TLB

Run from anything that gives you the evil thoughts that young men often have, but stay close to anything that makes you want to be right. Have faith and love, and enjoy the companionship of those who love the Lord and have pure hearts.

Father, from this day forward, I make a conscious choice to never objectify anyone again. We are Your creation and I will worship You and not the creation for it is idolatry. My eyes are only for my partner who I choose to love with all of my heart in all purity and godliness. I choose to please You in thought, feelings and purposes and I choose to be faithful to the partner that You have blessed me with. In Jesus name, Amen.

Step 4 Connection: Using the time a place named above, describe the reason why it is wrong to gawk at and lust over someone. Add this to your inventory.

[ ]

PARTNER CONNECT Once you have completed the exercise, ask your partner to share with you how they feel when you look too long at other people. Write down what they say.

OBJECTIFICATION

Don't Use Your Partner to Masturbate

Exercise 24

When first entering sexual addiction recovery, someone who has been in a program for a very, very long time said, "don't use your wife to masturbate with."

Why do you think someone would say that?

When somebody gets into sexual addiction recovery and they're used to sexual release on a regular basis to pornography or acting out with other people, it's very common for them to turn to their partner for their consistent sexual relief.
They will begin to project the porn they have viewed onto their wife.
This may not sound bad, except that you're engaging with your wife or partner not to connect with them in sexual intimacy, but for sexual release.

That means that you're treating your partner like an object, and that's anti-relational and destructive.

Think of a time when you objectified your partner and saw her solely as a sexual release. How would she feel about you treating her this way?

Now, to counter the objectification, list out **at least 5 things** that you cherish about your partner. This is called humanization. These are ways that you see her value, identity, and worth in who she is and her character.

Step 4 Connection: Being sexually used is a harm that will go unnoticed and unconfessed unless you do the work to uncover your patterns of acting out. Name a time you have "used" your partner sexually and what you selfishly gained out of doing it.

> **1 Thessalonians 4: 3,4 TLB**
>
> **For God wants you to be holy and pure and to keep clear of all sexual sin so that each of you will marry in holiness and honor- not in lustful passion as the heathen do, in their ignorance of God and his ways.**
>
> Father, I choose to be holy and pure. I will never use my partner for sexual release. I will give of myself to my partner so I can connect and be intimate with them. I will only do things that bring goodness so we can thrive as a couple and not merely co-exist. I choose to be a good steward of my relationship with my partner. In Jesus' name, Amen.

PARTNER CONNECT Share the 5 things you wrote down about what you cherish about your partner with them. Do not share any other parts of this exercise with your partner, as it will likely cause them pain to hear how you have objectified and used them.

Helping Your Partner Heal (Part 2)

THE FOUNDATIONS OF RECOVERY - PART 2 DIGGING DEEPER

 Exercise 25   # Wounding Agent vs Healing Agent

This exercise is specifically helpful in conflict. As guys, even though we may seem ok with conflict, we truly don't want to have conflict in a relationship.

We also call this the **two choices tool**. Re-wounding agent vs Healing Agent.

Re-wounding Agent: What are we saying or doing that is destructive, hurtful, holding back the growth? (We do these things to make ourselves feel safe)

Healing Agent: What am I doing or saying that is helpful and helping the other person feel safe?

Every time we are in conflict, we have this choice. We can still be a Healing Agent and get our point across to the other person.

Reflect on what you are **saying or doing** (or avoiding doing) that is either Re-Wounding or Healing your relationships.
List at least 7 for each.

Re-Wounding	Healing

> **Proverbs 15: 31, 32 AMPC**
>
> **The ear that listens to the reproof [that leads to or gives] life will remain among the wise. He who refuses and ignores instruction and correction despises himself, but he who needs reproof gets understanding.**
>
> Father, I do not want to do anything that is destructive or hurtful, or that holds back growth. Everything I do in thought, words, or deeds, from this day forward, will promote the creation of a beautiful relationship with my partner. I will give my partner many, many reasons to feel joy when they think about me or when they are spending time with me. I will do everything in my power to help our relationship thrive and bear the excellent fruit of faithfulness, honor, respect, and integrity. In Jesus' name, Amen.

Step 8/9 Connection: Use this list of Re-Wounding actions and cross-reference your steps 8/9 to see if there are any places you may need to include in your amends to those you have harmed. Write a prayer below to open your heart to giving amends for these ways you have been Re-Wounding others in conflict.

[ ]

PARTNER CONNECT Share what you are learning in this exercise with your partner. Ask them for their input. Write down what they say and use it to complete the exercise.

Coercive Sex - Cup of Tea

Exercise 26

Have you heard of the *cup of tea* analogy for sexual engagement? When you read "tea," equate that with sex.

It goes like this: you ask your partner if they would like a cup of tea. If they say yes, great, make them tea. If they say no, then don't.

Then, if they wanted tea, you may go heat the water, prepare the tea, and bring it to them, BUT

What if they say they now don't want a cup of tea?

Then don't make them drink it. Don't get annoyed. Now they don't want it. They have their own choice and that's ok for them to change it.

If they are unconscious, don't make them drink tea. They may have said yes earlier, BUT

It's taken too long to get the tea ready. Set the tea down, leave it for another day/time.

If they started drinking the tea and passed out while drinking it, don't keep pouring it down their throat.

If they wanted to drink tea last Saturday, that doesn't mean they want it every night.

If you can understand how ridiculous it is to expect or force someone else to drink tea,

it's the same with consent in sex. It's ok to say "no" and to be told "no."

When your partner says no to you, is it ok with you? Why should it be ok?

In what ways do you "prepare" the tea? Your partner needs to feel emotionally safe throughout the day to want to have sex. What ways can you choose to do that? Ask others in recovery how they create emotional safety for their partner.

> **Philippians 2:3 CEB**
>
> **Don't do anything for selfish purposes, but with humility think of others as better than yourselves.**
>
> Father, give me the grace to give my partner priority in all that I do, especially in the bedroom. You want the bed to be undefiled and the marriage to be pure. I treat my partner as holy and keep my covenant with my partner as sacred. Only then can we join together in unity and with Your blessing upon us. In Jesus' name, Amen.

THE FOUNDATIONS OF RECOVERY - PART 2 DIGGING DEEPER

What is your initiation statement? What do you say to your partner to offer tea? Write 1 or 2 sentences below that offer yourself sexually. Be ok with their "no." Say the sentences to yourself in the mirror.

[   ]

Step 9 Connection: In your sexual addiction inventory of harms done to others, consider if you have ever been coercive with sex. Have you pressured, complained, or been entitled about sex? What about with your partner? Complete an inventory entry for coercion and add it to your amends in Step 9.

Subject: Coercive Sex	What Happened	My Reaction	My Reason

PARTNER CONNECT Consult with your partner regarding your initiation statement. Ask them if this is an okay way to approach them, or if they would prefer something different. Take note of what they say.

HELPING YOUR PARTNER HEAL (PART 2)

Drama Triangle

Exercise 27

Drama refers to the feelings we have that are born from a physical, emotional, and spiritual need. Every person has a way that they will fall into drama with their partner. Stress induces the beginning of our role. Here are the 3 roles and ways to get out of them.

Rescuer: This is the desire to help someone, but it gets twisted to actually taking control of the situation. This is the "Mr. Fix It" persona. You may feel like, if you don't fix it, there is something wrong with you (shame) or you will be guilty of not having a solution to a problem.

Ways out: An example of how to get out of this role is to express understanding (see the Understanding Exercise). Encouraging the other person to seek a solution is a healthier alternative to providing one for them.

Persecutor: This persona will come out as critical, angry, and putting the other person down. Whether this is verbally or in your heart, this is destructive to the relationship.

Ways out: Be willing to listen to the other person and surrender the negative narrative you tell yourself about your partner. Take responsibility for your own actions, tone, demeanor, and words.

Victim: This role is a state of helplessness, powerlessness, and feeling misunderstood. Many traumas and wrongs committed towards us in our lives can give us an excuse to stay in this role or even act this role as a form of safety.

Ways out: Confess your victim mindset to another. Return to a state of thinking positively about yourself and others. Write down and express gratitudes for what is true about yourself and your partner.

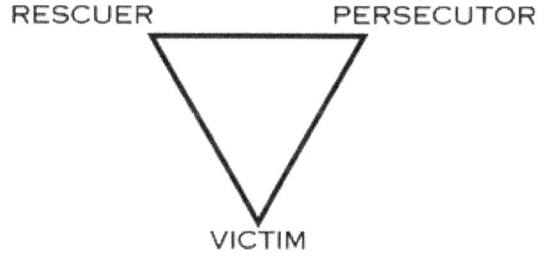

Which role do you sometimes take? Why?

Which role does your partner sometimes take? Why?

For your recovery, what actions can you take to exit your role and return to a place of love for your partner?

---

1 Corinthians 4: 18-20 AMP

Now some of you have become arrogant and pretentious, as though I were not coming to see you. But I will come to you, if the Lord is willing, and I will find out not just the talk of these arrogant people, but [evaluate] their [spiritual] power [whether they live up to their own claims]. For the Kingdom of God is not based on talk but on power.

Father, I will not fall into the negative roles of rescuer, persecutor, or victim. I will rely on healthy advice as to how to proceed with each situation that arises and watch Your delivering power at work in both myself and my partner. In Jesus' name, Amen.

Step 10 Connection:

Use opportunities throughout this week to make any amends necessary to you causing drama in your relationship. Record such instances here.

[ ]

PARTNER CONNECT You may share this exercise with your partner. Be cautious in sharing ways you think your partner participates in the Drama Triangle. It may be best to ask them about how they see their part.

Time Out Protocol

Exercise 28

The Time Out Protocol

The Time Out Protocol is the final piece of the three-part Communication Plan. There may be occasions when one or both partners become overwhelmed with emotions to the point that they can't function in a way that will support the health of the relationship. When someone is flooded with emotion, they may say or do things that attack the other person—adding even more pain to an already painful situation.

As a countermeasure to overwhelming emotions, the couple should develop a code word or a non-verbal sign that is an indicator that one of them needs to stop talking before they do more damage than good. Once a code word is spoken or a non-verbal sign is shown, the couple will disengage and agree to come back at a later time when things have calmed down. The couple should agree to the terms of time-out ahead of time and consider the Time Out Plan to be a contract between the two parties.

There are 5 main points to keep in mind when considering whether or not to call a time out:

1. USE THE CODE WORD or NON-VERBAL SIGN SPARINGLY. Time outs are considered an emergency option when all attempts at productive communication have failed. Understand that if either partner uses their code word or non-verbal sign to get out of conversations that they just don't want to deal with, they are hurting their partner. Using the code word or non-verbal sign to stonewall is also an improper use of a time out.

2. The request for time out should be honored. One partner should not try to goad the other into reengaging. The conversation needs to stop when time out is called. No attempting to have the last word.

3. When a code word or non-verbal sign has been used, agree on a time to reengage. Otherwise, one or both partners could feel neglected and abandoned. Typically, 20-30 minutes is recommended for a time out.

4. When a time out is taken, it is recommended that each person practice self-care. This means that an activity should be done to take the mind OFF of the present problem, as opposed to taking the time to stew about it and/or plan a rebuttal. Reading a book (not on the subject of the argument or infidelity), taking a shower/bath, or taking a walk are great activities to do. Time-outs do not work if either party uses the time to sit around and think about how angry they are or what they are going to say next in an effort to win the argument. The idea is to take your mind completely off the argument in order to give your flooded system a break.

5. When you come back from the time out, each partner needs to state at least one thing they appreciate about the other before resuming the conversation. When sharing feelings, use "I feel" statements as opposed to "you" statements. "You" statements come off as blaming. Blaming and/or criticizing will only make the problem worse. Focus on the solution as opposed to the problem(s) and be good listeners.

As with the Trigger Plan, the Time Out Plan should be developed at a calm moment.

To Do:

SIGN A COMMITMENT WITH YOUR PARTNER THAT FOR THE NEXT 90 DAYS YOU WILL TRY USINIG THIS

And return to this exercise to check if completed

> **Proverbs 29:11 AMP**
>
> **A [short sighted] fool always loses his temper and displays his anger, but a wise man [uses self-control and] holds it back.**
>
> Father, I choose to be wise and not a fool. I will not lose my temper or display a temper tantrum. I choose to be self-controlled and use the wisdom outlined in the Time Out Protocol. Fits only produce more damage than has already been incurred. Self-control will minimize damage and produce healing. Thank You for providing me the grace to be self-controlled. In Jesus' name, Amen.

PARTNER CONNECT Stonewalling is highly damaging to relationships. Identify at least two times in the past when you have stonewalled your partner. How did this damage your relationship? Ask them how this hurt them and write down what they say. Share your commitment to not use the Time Out Protocol to stonewall your partner when you don't feel like having a conversation. Commit to coming back to the conversation after the agreed-upon time has elapsed.

Demeanor Part 2

Exercise 29

If you are a wounding partner reading this and your partner is continuing to emotionally flood, chances are that you are engaging in behavior that is causing them to feel unsafe.

If you cannot or will not do everything you can to create a safe environment for your partner, any advances toward the restoration of the relationship will be slow to non-existent.

If you do not know what it is that you need to do, you should ask your partner at a time when they are not emotionally flooded. Typically, the things that make a wounded partner feel most safe are prioritizing the relationship, accountability for your actions and whereabouts, your availability to listen to them and meet their needs, and the consistency with which you behave in a manner that they interpret as loving.

Ask your partner and return here to reflect on their response and requests.

However, your partner may have other requirements. If these requirements are reasonable, agree to meet them. If you are not sure if they are reasonable, engage the help of a trained professional to help you understand.

As the wounding partner, earning back trust will require a great deal of patience on your part. You may tell your partner time and time again that you are "all in," but it takes much more than words to prove to them that you mean it. Rushing your partner toward "recovery" by complaining about their need to talk about it or shutting them down is not only unfair and inappropriate, but it comes across as controlling and uncaring.

You need to remember that their reactions are in response to your deception. It is going to take quite a while before they believe that you are no longer engaged in a double life. A word of caution: we see many wounding partners, especially intimacy avoidants, insist that their partner stop bringing the infidelity up in conversation. This will backfire if you are at all interested in the restoration of trust in the relationship.

Wounded partners who are shut down in this way share with us that they continue to feel a profound lack of trust and safety, even if they aren't voicing it. The only thing that shutting the conversation down does is ensure that the wounded partner does not share their feelings with you. This erodes trust even further over the long run and often results in the relationship ending.

Reflect:

Turn back to Demeanor Part 1. What actions have you been consistent in, inconsistent in, or need to begin to create safety for your partner?

Consistent	
Not Consistent	
Need to Begin	

> **1 Peter 1: 14, 15 ESV**
>
> **As obedient children, do not be conformed to the passions of your former ignorance, but as he who called you is holy, you also be holy in all your conduct.**
>
> Father, I choose to swap out that destructive belief system with Your righteous words and commands. Give me the grace to be holy in thought, word, and deed and in every circumstance. In Jesus' name, Amen.

HELPING YOUR PARTNER HEAL (PART 2)

The Cynical Script

Exercise 30

Our cynical script is the story that we tell ourselves that gives us the excuse or the reason to not connect or stay disconnected from our partner.

This is what we tell ourselves that gives us justification to create distance, or stay distant, from our partner.

List 5 lies or negative stories you tell yourself about your partner below:

1. _____
2. _____
3. _____
4. _____
5. _____

Proverbs 11:27 TLB

If you search for good, you will find God's favor; if you search for evil, you will find his curse.

If we have a cynical script of our partner, then we're looking at them like they're a problem. We're looking at the negative part about them. We're looking at where they fall short of the narrative that we create. The cynical script says they are a certain way, they're going to stay a certain way, and that they're against us. We must rewrite the cynical script. One way to do it is gratitude.

Father, I want Your favor. Thinking of my partner in a cynical way and making them the excuse for sinning is evil in Your sight. I will never place blame on anyone other than myself for seeking ways to be evil and carrying out wicked schemes. My partner is blameless in this and I will never lie to myself and make them the stumbling block for my cruel behavior. In Jesus' name, Amen.

List 5 gratitudes you tell yourself about your partner below:

1. _____
2. _____
3. _____
4. _____
5. _____

Tip: Snap your rubber band when a cynical script comes into your mind and pray gratitude in your heart.

Step 10 Connection: Compare your cynical scripts and gratitudes with a recovery partner. Pray with one another over the phone, for help to express gratitude instead of cynicism.

<u>**PARTNER CONNECT**</u> Do not share this exercise with your partner, as it will likely cause them pain.

Exercise 31 — Apology Language

Much like the well-known "Love Languages," we also have ways in which we would prefer to be apologized to when our partner has hurt us.

Your partner has a preferred way for you to make amends to them. Your partner needs to know that you fully understand the hurt you have caused and what was broken in that hurt.

Here are the 5 apology languages:

Expressing Regret	Using the words "I am sorry for…I regret hurting you by doing…"
Accepting Responsibility	Saying, "I was wrong. _____ was wrong to do to you. I take full responsibility for my actions."
Make Restitution	Asking, "What can I do right now to make it right?" If it's reasonable, do it.
Genuinely Repenting	Stating that you will work on it and being specific in what actions will be evidence of success or failure.
Requesting Forgiveness	Humbling yourself and admitting you're wrong with an invitation of "will you forgive me?"

Rank in order the 5 apology languages. This will show you how some ways of communication in an apology mean more to you. So, write **why** you would appreciate each form of an apology.

1. _____ Why… _____

2. _____ Why… _____

3. _____ Why… _____

4. _____ Why… _____

5. _____ Why… _____

Philippians 1: 9-11 CSB

And I pray that your love will keep on growing in knowledge and every kind of discernment so that you may approve the things that are superior and may be pure and blameless in the day of Christ, filled with the fruit of righteousness that comes through Jesus Christ to the glory and praise of God.

Father, as I write this apology letter, I ask that You assist me in putting healing words down on paper as I express my regret, the promise of acting responsibly, making restitution, genuinely repenting, and requesting forgiveness. I want my partner to know, from the depths of my heart, that I am a new creation. I am a person of absolute integrity and I will never dishonor our vows again. In Jesus' name, Amen.

HELPING YOUR PARTNER HEAL (PART 2)

ALL Step Connection: Share your apology languages with a recovery partner to prepare for sharing them with your partner.

Reflect below on why it would be important to know your partner's apology language.

[   ]

PARTNER CONNECT Once you have crafted your apology letter, with the help of a recovery partner, share it with your partner.

Exercise 32 **Reparations**

This is where we say that our actions speak louder than words ever can. Creating your list of reparations for your partner is an exercise of all the ways that you are repaying them for the pain you have caused with your SA/PA/IA behaviors. Fort his exercise, refer to the top 10 IA behaviors you have completed earlier in this exercise book AND your boundaries to remain sexually sober from your addiction of acting out.

Fill out the two tables below. The reparation/consequence actions are your ongoing responsibility for maintaining connection to your partner.

IA example: Action/Behavior is avoiding conflict around topics → Your reparation is to 4 nights out of the week use the empathy exercise to hear her pain.

SA/PA example: Action/Behavior is purposefully looking at sexually stimulating images → Reparation is one week of sleeping on the couch after massages for your partner nightly.

IA Action/Behavior	Reparation

Hebrews 12:11 ESV

For the moment all discipline seems painful rather than pleasant, but later it yields the peaceful fruit of righteousness to those who have been trained by it.

Father, as I put together this reparation plan with my partner, I ask for creative and effective consequences that will produce the fruit of righteousness in my life. In Jesus' name, Amen.

SA/PA Action/Behavior	Reparation

Step 8 Connection: Write a prayer around becoming willing to make amends. This prayer must include acknowledgement to God of the pain you have caused and continued to cause your partner. Surrender your life for God to heal, repair, and reconcile your relationship.

PARTNER CONNECT Share what you're working on with your partner. Ask them about actions they consider especially meaningful that will help you make amends. Do this before completing the exercise.

HELPING YOUR PARTNER HEAL (PART 2)

Love Language Sandwich   Exercise 33

The 5 love languages were first developed by Gary Chapman. They are...

1. Acts of Service
2. Receiving Gifts
3. Quality Time
4. Words of Affirmation
5. Physical Touch

These have been researched, used, and proven in practice for years in relationships. The goal of this exercise is to discover your partner's current top two love languages. Use this link to have your partner take a quiz. https://5lovelanguages.com/quizzes

My partner's top two love languages are

_____ and _____ .

What would prevent you from accommodating these love languages?

[   ]

Make a commitment in your running the marathon of recovery to do one of the top two languages in the morning and the other at night.

Brainstorm some ideas for how you can show each language to your partner. You can search for ways online, ask another in recovery, or have a conversation with your partner and ask them.

Love Language #1: _____	Love Language #2: _____
IDEAS: • • • • •	IDEAS: • • • • •

Philippians 2: 1b-8 TLB

Are your hearts tender and sympathetic at all? Then make me truly happy by loving each other and agreeing whole heartedly with each other, working together with one heart and mind and purpose. Don't be selfish; don't live to make a good impression on others. Be humble, thinking of others as better than yourself. Don't just think about your own affairs, but be interested in others, too, and in what they are doing. Your attitude should be the kind that was shown us by Jesus Christ, who, though he was God, did not demand and cling to his rights as God, but laid aside his mighty power and glory, taking the disguise of a slave and becoming like men. And he humbled himself even further, going so far as to actually die a criminal's death on a cross.

Father, I will not be pretentious but will seriously discover my partner's love language and incorporate it into our everyday lives. I will treat my partner better than I treat myself, just as Jesus modeled for me. In Jesus' name, Amen.

THE FOUNDATIONS OF RECOVERY - PART 2 DIGGING DEEPER

Now, rewrite which of them can be shown to your partner in the morning and which can be shown at night.

AM	PM
 • • • • •	 • • • •

Step 11 Connection: Recovery is a marathon. Write a prayer asking God to open your heart to show love with authenticity.

I, _____, commit to showing my partner, _____, love for the next 90 days using the following page to keep track.

Signature_____ Date_____

Check the boxes for each day you showed your partner love.

1	2	3	4	5	6	7	8	9	10
11	12	13	14	15	16	17	18	19	20
21	22	23	24	25	26	27	28	29	30
31	32	33	34	35	36	37	38	39	40
41	42	43	44	45	46	47	48	49	50
51	52	53	54	55	56	57	58	59	60
61	62	63	64	65	66	67	68	69	70
71	72	73	74	75	76	77	78	79	80
81	82	83	84	85	86	87	88	89	90

Importance of Dates

Exercise 34

Weekly dates are essential for building and keeping a strong relationship. In Bradford Wilcox and Jeffery Dew's study "The Date Night Opportunity: What Does Couple Time Tell Us About the Potential Value of Date Nights?" There are 5 reasons to make time for weekly dates.

1. Good Communication: On dates, you want to practice having open communication. It must be viewed as something you are always improving in.
2. Novelty: Doing something new with your partner can create excitement and fresh memories in the relationship.
3. Romantic Love: This is the aspect that can spark a memory of why you fell in love and the things that you're grateful for about your partner.
4. Commitment: By consistently planning dates, you will grow closer in trust and accountability for nurturing the relationship.
5. Destress: Making memories and having fun can be a much-needed break from discussion about the hard topics such as infidelity, sex addiction, and intimacy avoidance.

Suggestion: You alternate who decides where and what you will do on the date. This gives both partners the chance to plan new and different things for the two of you to have fun doing together.

Pitfalls: Last minute planning, dates you know your partner won't enjoy, being busy or distracted on the date, being inconsistent in planning dates every week, and of course sex addiction behaviors such as ogling or flirting can re-wound your partner (See *Battling Objectification* for SA tips).

Which of the 5 reasons are you the weakest in? Why?

> **1 Corinthians 7:3-5 NIRV**
>
> **A husband should satisfy his wife's needs. And a wife should satisfy her husband's needs. The wife's body does not belong only to her. It also belongs to her husband. In the same way, the husband's body does not belong only to him. It also belongs to his wife. You shouldn't stop giving yourselves to each other. You might possibly do this when you both agree to it. And you should only agree to it to give yourselves time to pray. Then you should come together again. In that way, Satan will not tempt you when you can't control yourselves.**
>
> Father, it is our heart's desire to build and keep a strong relationship. We are good stewards of our relationship with each other, and we will thoughtfully and deliberately plan our time together and enjoy each other! We intentionally give ourselves fully to each other to become more and more intimate. As we grow together, our love for each other will deepen with each passing day. In Jesus' name, Amen.

THE FOUNDATIONS OF RECOVERY - PART 2 DIGGING DEEPER

Which of the pitfalls have you fallen into? Recall how it made your partner feel for each.

Come up with ideas for dates over the next 13 weeks. Identify different places to eat and enjoy a fun activity. Call others in recovery for ideas. Research places to eat.

Week	Food	Activity	Date
1			__/__/__
2			__/__/__
3			__/__/__
4			__/__/__
5			__/__/__
6			__/__/__
7			__/__/__
8			__/__/__
9			__/__/__
10			__/__/__
11			__/__/__
12			__/__/__
13			__/__/__

Step 2 Connection: Write a prayer expressing your desire for your relationship to grow and heal, mentioning dates as a way to do so.

Warning Signs

SA/PA Warning Signs

Exercise 35

Since recovery is an ongoing process, you will need to be vigilant in what you think, say, do, and believe. Every thought can lead to a path of action. Every belief will manifest in some way in your relationships.

Instructions

On the left-hand side of the table, list the attitudes, thoughts, behaviors, and beliefs that are warning signs to you that you might be headed for a relapse into sexually addictive behavior or pornography use. On the right-hand side, write down strategies for coping with these.

Attitudes, Thoughts, Behaviors, and Beliefs *Warning Signs*	Strategies to Cope

Malachi 2: 13-16 AMP

This is another thing you do: you cover the altar of the Lord with tears, with [your own] weeping and sighing, because the Lord no longer regards your offering or accepts it with favor from your hand. But you say, "Why [does he reject it]?" Because the Lord has been a witness between you and the wife of your youth, against whom you have dealt treacherously. Yet she is your marriage companion and the wife of your covenant [made by your vows]. But not one has done so who has a remnant of the Spirit. And what did that one do while seeking a godly offspring? Take heed then to your spirit, and let no one deal treacherously against the wife of your youth. "For I hate divorce" says the Lord God of Israel, "And him who covers his garment with wrong and violence," says the Lord of Hosts. "Therefore keep watch on your spirit, so that you do not deal treacherously [with your wife].'

Father, with all of my heart, I want Your favor in my life and upon my relationship with my partner. I dedicate my body to You as a living sacrifice, acceptable and holy to You, Lord. Give me a deep abhorrence of sexual sin. Give me the grace to never, ever deal treacherously with my partner by heaping upon them the violence of any type of sexual infidelity. In Jesus' name, Amen.

WARNING SIGNS

Price of Addiction

Exercise 36

In this exercise, we will focus in on the time, energy, and ultimately financial cost of your sexual addiction. The purpose of doing this is to reveal just how much your addiction has cost you.

Age Range	Acting Out Behaviors	Hours in Behavior Weekly	Your Average Hourly Wage	Total Price of Addiction
5-10				
11-20				
21-30				
31-40				
41-50				
51-60				
61-70				
71-80				
80+				

Total Weekly Hours _____   Price Of Addiction _____

Miscellaneous Costs

Legal Fees _____

Therapy   _____

Child

Support   _____

Other

_____ _____

_____ _____

Total Price Of Addiction _____

Step 5 Connection: Confess the cost to another in recovery. List the feelings you have about the price of your addiction here. Then, write the price and time lost on a flash card and place it into your wallet where you keep cash and cards.

> **1 Peter 2:11 AMP Beloved, I urge you as aliens and strangers [in this world] to abstain from the sensual urges [those dishonorable desires] that wage war against the soul.**
>
> Father, the price of addiction is too high to pay and the damage from it is too much to bear. But, in You, we can trust. You will exceed all that we can ask or think. Thank you for Your loving kindness and tender mercies. In Jesus' name, Amen.

Tips to Avoid Relapse

Exercise 37

Here we prepare our recovery journey for all the situations where we'll be tempted to act out in our sexual addiction. For everything from mental fantasy to paid sex, you can set up plans to avoid temptations. Each section below has three lines, but use more if you need to. Remember: temptation is a powerless thing, but the choice to run from your addiction is in your power.

1. **Cravings are temporary.** Distract yourself with activities or make phone calls until the cravings pass.

   a.

   b.

   c.

2. **Don't think you have it beat.** It isn't uncommon for people to relapse after years of sobriety if they become complacent or make excuses like, "one time won't hurt me."

   a.

   b.

   c.

3. **Avoid risky situations.** Avoid risky situations, such as not having adequate blocking software, using your phone late at night, or watching visually stimulating movies or videos—even if they aren't "technically" pornography.

   a.

   b.

   c.

4. **Remember relapse doesn't start with off-limits behavior.**
   Relapse starts to happen the moment you make excuses that put yourself in risky situations. This is usually long before you act out. Many addicts report having relapsed after they were "riding the line" for days or weeks.

   a.

   b.

   c.

> **1 Peter 5: 8, 9a CEB**
>
> **Be clear headed. Keep alert. Your accuser, the devil, is on the prowl like a roaring lion seeking someone to devour. Resist him, standing firm in the faith.**
>
> Father, I am equipped with the truth. Cravings are temporary. I will not make excuses to fall into sin. I will avoid all risky situations. By Your grace, I am always alert, and I resist every urge, every craving. I resist every excuse. I am strong in the Lord and in the power of Your might! In Jesus' name, Amen.

5. **Don't view relapse as a complete failure.** If you slip up, own it. Don't use it as an excuse to fall back into old patterns.

a.

b.

c.

Step 1 Connection: You may be powerless over the temptations to relapse, although there are day-to-day choices that you have power over. What choices will you make to avoid relapse this week?

PARTNER CONNECT With your partner, share the activities you have identified to fight cravings. Who are you going to be accountable to?

IA Warning Signs

Exercise 38

Since recovery is an ongoing process, you will need to be vigilant in what you think, say, do, and believe. Every thought can lead to a path of action. Every belief will manifest in some way in your relationships.

Instructions

On the left-hand side of the table, list the attitudes, thoughts, behaviors, and beliefs that are warning signs to you that you might be headed for a relapse into IA behavior. On the right-hand side, write down strategies for coping with these.

Attitudes, Thoughts, Behaviors, and Beliefs *Warning Signs*	Strategies to Cope

Proverbs 5: 15-21 CEV

You should be faithful to your wife, just as you take water from your own well. And don't be like a stream from which just any woman may take a drink. Save yourself for your wife and don't have sex with other women. Be happy with the wife you married when you were young. She is beautiful and graceful, just like a deer; you should be attracted to her and stay deeply in love. Don't go crazy over a woman who is unfaithful to her own husband! The Lord sees everything, and he watches us closely.

Father, I will not be Intimacy avoidant with my partner. This is an abomination to You! You demand that I be morally pure in spirit, soul, and body. I will not spread myself around, checking others out, expressing my attraction, and giving them the impression that I am available for them. You demand that I work hard to stay attractive to my partner, so they may stay attractive to me. You demand that I guard my emotions so that I remain deeply in love with my partner and they, in turn, remain deeply in love with me. Give me the grace to work hard at this godly mandate and to never deviate from this path. In Jesus' name, Amen.

PARTNER CONNECT Ask your partner for their input into your IA warning signs.

How to Spot IA Behaviors

Exercise 39

A big question we get is: "How do I know if the behavior I'm experiencing is related to IA?"

Not every behavior is related to IA.

We all have bad days.

There are 6 questions that you can ask that help determine whether it was IA or not:

1. Was this behavior directed at the partner only? If so, what was I feeling?
2. Was the behavior effective at creating distance? If so, in which way?
3. Do I use this behavior repetitively? If so, how often per week?
4. Did the behavior move us closer together or further apart? If so, in what ways?
5. Did the behavior occur after sexual, emotional, or spiritual connection? If so, explain.
6. When confronted by the behavior, did the IA analyze the situation or grow defensive?

Over the course of the next week, be mindful of your behaviors. Recall that there are 40 types of behaviors of IA, which we have given you in a previous exercise. In the table below, analyze your behavior using the 6 questions above.

Behavior: _____

1. _____
2. _____
3. _____
4. _____
5. _____
6. _____

Behavior: _____

1. _____
2. _____
3. _____
4. _____
5. _____
6. _____

> **1 Corinthians 10:13 AMP**
>
> **No temptation [regardless of its source] has overtaken or enticed you that is not common to the human experience [nor is any temptation unusual or beyond human resistance]; but God is faithful [to His word-He is compassionate and trustworthy], and he will not let you be tempted beyond your ability [to resist], but along with the temptation He [has in the past and is now and] will [always] provide the way out as well, so that you will be able to endure it [without yielding, and will overcome temptation with joy].**
>
> Father, it is much easier to stop temptation when it is just a thought or whim than it is to stop when I give into it fully. Help me to recognize when I am falling into the trap of Intimacy Avoidance. Open the eyes of my understanding! Allow me to see the error of my ways and to run from the very thought of sin as fast as I can! I never want to experience the consequences of IA in my life again, and I never want my partner to experience the pain of IA from me again! In Jesus' name, Amen.

THE FOUNDATIONS OF RECOVERY - PART 2 DIGGING DEEPER

Behavior: _____

1. _____
2. _____
3. _____
4. _____
5. _____
6. _____

Step 11 Connection: Write a prayer and surrender the thoughts, feelings, and subsequent behaviors you still struggle with. Open your heart in honesty and dependency for God's help.

PARTNER CONNECT Ask for your partner's input to help you create your list of IA behaviors.

WARNING SIGNS

Middle of the Roof

Exercise 40

Have you ever stood on a roof? Anyone who has, knows the safest place to stand is at the peak with a foot on either side. Picture this analogy for your recovery. There are actions, behaviors, and temptations that would be considered "edging," walking towards the edge of the roof. If we aren't careful, they will lead to relapse or avoiding intimacy with our partners. Our goal in recovery is to stay in the "middle of the roof." Falling off the roof would be harmful towards yourself and others.

There are aspects of our lives that are in our control and others that are out of our control.

Identifying the actions, behaviors, and temptations for both is essential to staying in the "middle of the roof."

Examples:

In your control: what you watch for entertainment, what you eat/drink, when you go to bed, making a phone call, where you drive, who you spend your time with, how you manage your stress (*self-care plan*)

Not in your control: your thoughts, other's perspectives/opinions of you or in general, your feelings, your memories, your past

What actions, behaviors, or temptations walk you towards the edge and eventually falling off the roof? Organize these into the table below:

In your control	Not in your control

How does your partner feel when you "edge" towards relapse in SA or avoid intimacy? How would you and your partner benefit from your recovery in these areas?

Proverbs 27:12 AMP

A prudent man sees evil and hides himself and avoids it, But the naive [who are easily misled] continue on and are punished [by suffering the consequences of sin].

Father, give me grace to be prudent and keep me from straying from Your word and Your standards. Open my eyes to traps ahead. Give me the courage to run away from those temptations and honor You and my partner. In Jesus' name, Amen.

THE FOUNDATIONS OF RECOVERY - PART 2 DIGGING DEEPER

Step 1 Connection: Over a phone call, share the things out of your control with another in recovery. Record similarities you both share in the space below.

[ ]

PARTNER CONNECT In order to complete your assignment, you need to ask your partner about how they feel when you engage in behaviors that "edge" you toward relapse. Also, ask them how they would benefit from your recovery in these areas. Record their answers.

Anger and Resentment Letter   Exercise 41

We all have anger and resentment. Most of us have heard the expression, "resentment is like drinking poison and expecting the other person to die." We know that resentment is corrosive by nature, both personally and relationally. It's time to process this so we're not carrying it around. Here's a way to do that.

You're going to write a one-to-two-page letter, expressing your intense and specific anger, resentment, frustration, etc. This isn't *dear honey*. This is sharing all the things that they've done to you, ways they've hurt you or caused you pain. When we're resentful, we hold onto and focus on situations out of context. In this exercise, you're just going to write what you dwell on in anger outside of context so that you can really get it out.

You will write separate anger letters toward the areas below. List out your resentments for each before their letters.

1. Wounded Partner
2. Yourself
3. Mother &/or Father
4. God/Higher Power

1. Anger/Resentment towards partner

2. Anger/Resentment towards yourself

3. Anger/Resentment towards mom and dad

4. Anger/Resentment towards God/Higher Power

Hebrews 12:15 TLB

Look after each other so that not one of you will fail to find God's best blessings. Watch out that no bitterness takes root among you, for as it springs up it causes deep trouble, hurting many in their spiritual lives.

Father, in my assignment, I ask that You enlighten me and shed Your light on the areas of my heart that are defiled by anger and resentment. As I compose these letters, I will empty my soul of this bitterness so that I will not cause deep trouble or harm the spiritual lives of others. Thank You for all of Your grace and help. In Jesus' name, Amen.

WARNING SIGNS

I write this to **express my anger/resentment towards** _____

I write this to **express my anger/resentment towards** _____

WARNING SIGNS

I write this to **express my anger/resentment towards** _____

I write this to **express my anger/resentment towards** _____

_____
_____
_____
_____
_____
_____
_____
_____
_____
_____
_____
_____
_____
_____
_____
_____
_____
_____
_____
_____
_____
_____
_____
_____
_____
_____
_____
_____
_____
_____
_____
_____
_____

WARNING SIGNS

Releasing Anger and Resentment

Exercise 42

After you're done with your letters, you are going to take each resentment, frustration, etc., line by line and break it apart.

You will break apart all of your letters into sentence statements for each of the following:

a. The picture (What specific memory or image comes to your mind?)
b. The movie (What does the scene look like? What is the context of the anger? Why?)
c. The truth (Describe the conflict)
d. What you're going to do to let it go (Action sentence)
e. How are you going to release it emotionally?
f. How are you going to release it through physical activity? (explain)

1 Peter 2:23 AMP

While being reviled and insulted, He did not revile or insult in return; while suffering, He made no threats [of vengeance], but kept entrusting Himself to Him who judges fairly.

Father, as this exercise demands of me, I will take each resentment and frustration apart. I choose to release every angry emotion and every frustrating circumstance. I will do it as thoroughly as possible. Thank You, Jesus, for Your amazing example of forgiveness and mercy. Father, thank You for the blood of Jesus that cleanses me from all unrighteousness. In Jesus' name, Amen.

Anger/Resentment Towards Partner	
The picture	
The movie	
The truth	
What I'm going to do to let it go?	
How are you going to release it emotionally?	
How are you going to release it through physical activity?	

Anger/Resentment Towards Yourself	
The picture	
The movie	
The truth	

THE FOUNDATIONS OF RECOVERY - PART 2 DIGGING DEEPER

What I'm going to do to let it go?	
How are you going to release it emotionally?	
How are you going to release it through physical activity?	

Anger/Resentment Towards Mom/Dad	
The picture	
The movie	
The truth	
What I'm going to do to let it go?	
How are you going to release it emotionally?	
How are you going to release it through physical activity?	

Anger/Resentment Towards God/Higher Power	
The picture	
The movie	
The truth	
What I'm going to do to let it go?	
How are you going to release it emotionally?	
How are you going to release it through physical activity?	

WARNING SIGNS

Step 7 Connection: In order to be prepared to ask God/Higher Power to remove our character defects, we must be honest. This is especially true about anger/resentment. Let the walls come down. You are accepted even if you feel anger. Share this anger towards God with another this week and pray together over it. Reflect on the way it felt to be honest to God and another person about this anger.

Exercise 43 — Affair Types

<u>The One Night Stand</u> – opportunity and convenience. If this was you then you need to set boundaries with business, with other women, and with travel. Identify a good peer group that has the same values.

- This results in loose boundaries
    - Carelessness is involved
- Pride
- Alcohol

<u>Love Struck</u> – This is the limerence affair. You think that you are in love and are willing to give up everything that is important to you for this infatuation. Your thinking is distorted in terms of who the affair partner was and who your partner really is.

- Obsession – pursuit of happiness that takes over everything
- In your Life Plan you have an obligation to stay committed, and you have goals that are really important to you.
- Obviously, you need to terminate the relationship.
- The third choice is about choosing God over the affair partner and your spouse.
    - How do you have a life of meaning and purpose beyond just seeking happiness?
    - *31 Reasons* is a good resource

<u>Sexual Addiction</u> – this is a physiological, chemical, and escalating condition. If there is a hint that you have an addiction, then assume that that is the case. Do the 12 steps. This will keep you from relapse.

- Where you are weak you can be strong. You will have deeper relationships than you thought possible with the mentor/support community
- If you are an addict, you will 100% relapse
- Work a strong recovery program into your Life Plan
    - Give back to others who struggle with this addiction.

<u>Wanting Your Cake & Eating It Too</u> – this is more about entitlement and possibly cultural. Maybe family members did it and you have a "that's just the way things are done" mentality

- In your Life Plan, do your own work on personal integrity. Find a community of people who want to be monogamous and faithful. Don't hang out with peers who think it is ok to have an affair.

<u>Emotional Affair</u> – you look to another person to fulfill your emotional goals. You let someone else into your marriage life.

- "we are just friends" – if this is hurting the boundary around your marriage, it needs to end.
- In your Life Plan, make these kinds of relationships not an option. Make your marriage your priority.
    - Find appropriate places to get those emotional needs met.
    - Emotional affairs are just physical affairs waiting to happen.
    - What habits and ways of being do you need to change?

WARNING SIGNS

<u>Love Addiction</u>: you become attached to them without even knowing them. You compulsively continue to involve yourself in relationships that aren't good for you.

SLAA – Sex and Love Addicts Anonymous

Think about what needs to be in your life plan to stay faithful.

Let's do what is necessary to protect you and your family from future hurt.

> **Proverbs 6:32 TLB**
>
> **But the man who commits adultery is an utter fool, for he destroys his own soul.**
>
> Father, every kind of fornication/adultery is an abomination to You. Give me the grace to hate this sin as much as You do. I will shed off this snakeskin of evil and walk as a godly individual with purity. I declare that I am a whole person, and every layer of lust and entitlement is removed from my soul. I am the righteousness of Christ Jesus and sin has no place in me anymore! In Jesus' name, Amen.

Step 7 Connection: **Write a letter as if it's 5 years from now: "How I relapsed."** Explain how an affair would likely occur. Include the pain it would cause all parties involved. Finish it with a prayer asking for God's protection from any future affairs.

_____
_____
_____
_____
_____
_____
_____
_____
_____
_____
_____
_____
_____
_____
_____
_____

<u>**PARTNER CONNECT**</u> Share what you wrote about the steps necessary to ensure safety with your partner. Ask for their input in case you missed anything. Write down what they tell you.

Exercise 44: Cascade Towards Betrayal

Here we will look at a list of situations, conflicts, and evidence that show a relationship is headed towards betrayal. Because many of those using this exercise book have already committed a betrayal, much of this exercise should cause you to feel guilt. This guiltiness is meant to help you come out of hiding, recover from the very nature of your brokenness, and be honest.

Between the 1st step (turning away from or against your partner) and crossing the line to infidelity at the 20th step (Not dismissing alternative relationships), we find that Intimacy Avoidants will get all the way to step 19. Betrayal is happening even if it doesn't cross over into an inappropriate relationship with someone other than our partner.

Out of the table below, **circle** the Cascade towards betrayal evidence that are a part of your story.

Turning Away or Against	Partner: "Not there for me"	Flooding/Physiological Arousal	(4) Conflict with repair no longer working
(5) Avoidance of Conflict, then Blowups	(6) Keeping Secrets from Others	(7) Negative Comparisons between Partner and others	(8) Attempts to Connect Decline
(9) Investment in Relationship Declines	(10) Confiding in Others, not the Partner	(11) Less Sacrificial for Relationship	(12) Maximizing Negative traits of Partner
(13) Minimizing Positive Traits of Partner	(14) Trashing on instead of Cherishing	(15) Slandering Partner	(16) Practicing Resentment v. Gratitude
(17) Loneliness in Relationship	(18) Little to no Sexuality, romance, fun, play or courtship	(19) Less Pro-Relationship Thoughts	(20) Not dismissing alternative relationships
(21) Walls with partner, Windows with others	(22) Keeping more and more Secrets from Partner	(23) Actively Turning towards others Emotionally	(24) Crossing Boundaries, Real betrayal unfolds

Gottman-Rusbult-Glass

In another color, identify any evidence that you've still been displaying lately. What are you valuing more than the relationship for 3 of these (Step 4 Connection)?

Evidence	What am I valuing more than the relationship?
1.	
2.	

Ezekiel 36:26,27 AMP

Moreover, I will give you a new heart and put a new spirit within you, and I will remove the heart of stone from your flesh and give you a heart of flesh. I will put my spirit within you and cause you to walk in my statutes, and you will keep my ordinances and do them.

Father, remove from me this stony, cold, detached and intimacy-avoidant heart. This is not how a child of God thinks, feels, or acts. Place a heart in me that is tender toward you and toward my partner. Help my thoughts, feelings, and purposes to align with Yours. In Jesus' name, Amen.

PARTNER CONNECT Be sure to share what you have identified with your partner. If they have identified other evidence that you weren't aware of, write down what they say.

Marathon of Recovery

Self-Care Plan

Exercise 45

Your recovery from SA or IA is highly affected by what you do on a day-to-day basis. This exercise is meant to create a space for you to explore the actions and activities you can take, starting today, to keep yourself in a healthy mindset for yourself, your family, your friends, and above all others, God. Three lines are available for each section, but don't stop with just 3. Create a plan for taking care of your heart, mind, body, and spirit.

1. Activities that support my physical well-being

   a.

   b.

   c.

2. Activities that support my spiritual well-being

   a.

   b.

   c.

3. Activities that support my emotional/mental well-being

   a.

   b.

   c.

4. Activities that support my social well-being

   a.

   b.

   c.

Romans 12: 1-2 TLB And so, dear brothers, I plead with you to give your bodies to God. Let them be a living sacrifice, holy- the kind you can accept. When you think of what he has done for you, is this too much to ask? Don't copy the behavior and the customs of this world, but be a new and different person with a fresh newness in all you do and think. Then you will learn from your own experience how his ways will really satisfy you.

Father, taking care of myself is an investment. It demonstrates to You that I respect the body that You gave to me. It proves that I am a good steward. And if I take care of myself, I will also take care of others. In Jesus' name, Amen.

THE FOUNDATIONS OF RECOVERY - PART 2 DIGGING DEEPER

5. Activities that support my active recovery

   a.

   b.

   c.

ALL Step Connection: Make 3 phone calls and record ideas below from their self-care plans. We are stronger together in recovery.

| 1. | 2. | 3. |

Self-Care Schedule

Exercise 46

Use your self-care worksheet to plan and create a schedule of activities, the days you will do them, and times.

Be diligent with these plans and on the same page with your partner. This can involve times when you need a quiet space to center yourself after a long day at work, exercise, prayer, and family activities, to name a few. Agree with your partner on durations of anything you plan to do without them on your own.

Activity	Day	Time

ALL Step Connection: *Bookend* these self-care activities over phone calls. With your recovery partners, share your ideas and ask them what they do for self-care.

> **Mark 1:35 Very early in the morning, while it was still dark, Jesus got up, left the house and went off to a solitary place, where he prayed.**
>
> Father, even Jesus kept a schedule and You were always first on his schedule. If my relationship with you is healthy, and I take care of all other aspects of my life, then You will bless the works of my hands and I will remain healthy and strong. In Jesus' name, Amen.

Flawed and Loved

Exercise 47

Throughout the rest of your recovery journey, you will have times when you will doubt if you are worth being loved after all the pain you have caused. This is a flawed, broken, and shameful reaction to memories and mistakes on a weekly basis.

This exercise is meant to keep your heart free from the shame and doubts you have about being loved by your partner. It is understandable to feel those feelings, yet they are a counter against your openness and intimacy with your partner.

Here's the exercise we would like you to do with your partner.

1. Sit in chairs facing one another. Give eye contact. Clear your mind. Hold hands.
2. Say "I am flawed"
3. Partner replies, "and I love you"
4. Repeat for 1 minute
5. Rest for 15-30 seconds
6. Repeat Steps 2-5 for a second time
7. Repeat Steps 2-5 a third time
8. Give each other a hug and kiss if comfortable too.

In the table below, record your feelings after each time you use this exercise in the next week. Repeat this exercise specifically when you are feeling like you are unlovable.

Day	Your Feelings	Your Partner's Feelings
1		
2		
3		
4		
5		
6		
7		

Ephesians 4:32 KJV

And be ye kind to one another, tenderhearted, forgiving one another, even as God for Christ's sake hath forgiven you.

Father, I know that I am flawed. I thank You that my partner knows I am flawed and loves me anyways, warts and all! My partner is like You, Lord. Thank you for Your loving kindness and tender mercies towards me. Thank You for a partner who shows loving kindness and tender mercies toward me, too. I ask You to give me the grace to never disappoint You or my partner ever again. In Jesus' name, Amen.

Step 11 Connection: Write a prayer giving up the shame and lies that you are unlovable. Accept your brokenness. Accept your need for God to open and soften your heart to receive love.

<u>PARTNER CONNECT</u> Ask your partner if they are open to doing this exercise with you. If they are, practice it every day with them.

Daily 10ᵗʰ Step Inventory

Exercise 48

These next two pages are meant to be printed and filled out throughout the marathon of recovery you are now entering. The point of the final 3 steps is that it's not over with. Our brokenness is only mended over a lifetime. For most of us, most of our lives have already been spent in either a sexual/porn addiction and/or intimacy avoidance. Here we will have no step connection at the end because this entire exercise can be cross-referenced with the questions you answer in the 10ᵗʰ step.

General Recovery

Resentments?
Anger?
Contempt towards
- Partner:
- Other family member:
- Other family member:
- Colleague:

Dishonesty with myself? Others?
Fear?
Gratitude list for today?
- Partner:
- Other family member:
- Other family member:
- Colleague:

New understandings/insights?

My SA/IA program

What were lust-based decisions I made?

What recovery-based decisions are people making in my SA program?

Love Language sandwich

(AM- _____ 1ˢᵗ love language,

PM- _____ 2ⁿᵈ love language)

Replace these with some of the 40 ways, or from our new list

Am I busy, choosing work over my relationship?

Blame shifting?

Defending/explaining?

Playing the victim?

> **2 Peter 1:10 AMP** Therefore, believers, be all the more diligent to make certain about his calling and choosing you [be sure that your behavior reflects and confirms your relationship with God]; for by doing these things [actively developing these virtues], you will never stumble [in your spiritual growth and will live a life that leads others away from sin]...
>
> Father, open the eyes of my understanding as I go through this checklist. Help me see the areas I need to change in and give me the wisdom of how to activate that change. I can do all things through Christ Jesus! Through Jesus, I can overcome all obstacles and be victorious because of the great price He paid for me! In Jesus' name, Amen.

Expecting others to read my mind?

Cynical Script?

% Choose Door B - Self regulate, good people, boundary, what can I do for them?

Did I do bookwork?

Did I do an SA/IA meeting in the last seven days?

Did I make a recovery phone call or texts?

Did I do dailies, check in, sexual agreement?

What could I have done differently?

My Work/Life/Self-Care

Hours worked:

Did I get 7 hrs. of sleep?

Did I play games or just sit in my chair for at least 15 minutes?

Did I get a full nonworking lunch?

Did I get two full days off from both offices in the last seven days?

Did I get 2 Matt evenings in the last seven days?

Did I work the number of hours that would keep me at/under 42hrs work, 18hrs/school?

Did I do recovery bookwork?

Did I do a WA meeting in the last seven days?

Did I make a recovery phone call or text?

What could I have done differently in any of the categories (reflection practice)?

PARTNER CONNECT Share what you learned about your work/life balance with your partner. Share the areas you identified as needing improvement.

MARATHON OF RECOVERY

The Hot Seat

Exercise 49

Note: This is a protocol we use in My Becoming Well Workgroups

Being In The Hot Seat

- Purpose of the hot seat is for you to get feedback on something that your relationship is struggling with
- This is not to tear you down but build you up
- Guys need to have two topics ready: On SA or IA recovery
- If a guy doesn't come prepared, the 20 minutes is still given to that participant to dig into how the relationship is going and get feedback.
- Time Frame: 3 min. share, 15 min feedback, & 2 min. action plan
- Victim Mindset is avoided

Giving Feedback

- Take Notes, Be Engaged, listen
- Think of a question that will dig deeper and uncover what's holding them back
- Target questions/sharpening for what actions they can take
- ALL feedback given is gentle with praises and sharpening purpose.
- NO feedback is to make the topic about you. ALL other members in the group are to ask questions for more details, praise/encourage them for sharing, OR give them a sharpening suggestion.
- Free Form - Any member in the group can jump in and start giving feedback during the 13-minute feedback loop.

Outcomes

- The guy in the Hot Seat states and personally records Action Items and/or Takeaways.
- Guys should be coming away from this with action items.
- The group is responsible for following up with the guy in the

Hot Seat to keep them accountable to their action items. Phone calls are made to keep accountability at its highest.

- Guys are meant to leave the Hot Seat feeling empowered relationally.

Name two topics related to either your sexual addiction OR intimacy Avoidance that you would want feedback on and bring to The Hot Seat. Why did you choose these topics?

> **2 Timothy 4:2 AMP**
>
> **Be ready when the time is right and even when it is not [keep your sense of urgency, whether the opportunity seems favorable or unfavorable, whether convenient or inconvenient, whether welcome or unwelcome]; correct [those who err in doctrine or behavior], warn [those who sin], exhort and encourage [those who are growing towards spiritual maturity], with inexhaustible patience and [faithful] teaching.**
>
> Father, the Hot Seat is a tool to help me in the areas where my relationship is struggling. Give me the grace to humbly present myself before my peers and my counselors, so that I can be accurate in defining my struggles. Give me the grace to hear each person's perspective, so that I can be sharper and more successful in my relationship with my partner. Help me to appreciate every person's advice. They want the best for me, and I ask You to bless them as they encourage me along in such an important endeavor. In Jesus' name, Amen.

| 1. | Why? |
| 2. | |

THE FOUNDATIONS OF RECOVERY - PART 2 DIGGING DEEPER

ALL Step Connection: One of the core purposes of the step process is to help build a community that relies upon one another, builds each other up, and holds one another accountable.

Describe how one of the steps relates to The Hot Seat.

[ ]

PARTNER CONNECT Using your best self-reflection skills, share at least one thing you learned about yourself during the hot seat with your partner.

Recovery Travel Plan

Exercise 50

Written by Jeff H. from Oregon

Oftentimes when we travel, vacation, or get out of our normal routine, we can have problems. It's important to have a plan when we break our routine. Without a plan, we can flounder and white-knuckle our way through our trip. We may not be able to do recovery the same exact way as when we are home, but with a good plan we can stay close to God and have a successful trip. Below is a worksheet to think through our trip, make decisions, and come up with a good plan. This only works if we implement our plan and put it into action when we are out.

Morning Prayer – The plan for my morning prayer is _____

Daily Reading – The plan for my daily reading is _____

Meetings – I will or will not be attending meetings during the trip? _____

Phone Calls – I will or will not be making calls during the trip? _____

Other Support – What are other ways I can have fellowship or get support during my travels? _____
_____

What are potential triggers I am anticipating during my travels? _____
_____

What is my plan to handle the triggers?
_____
_____

Accountability – Who will I be accountable to during my trip? (This is at least one person I will keep in the loop as to how I am doing) _____
_____

Other limitations – Are there other things I should limit or make a decision to withhold while I am on my trip? (Stuff like alcohol, watching TV alone etc.) _____
_____

What is my emergency action plan in case I get off track? What adjustments will I make if I have more than one bad day and can't get back on track? _____
_____

> **Ephesians 5: 15-17 AMP**
>
> **Therefore see that you walk carefully [living life with honor, purpose, and courage; shunning those who tolerate and enable evil], not as the unwise, but as wise [sensible, intelligent, discerning people], making the very most of your time [on earth, recognizing and taking advantage of each opportunity and using it with wisdom and diligence], because the days are [filled with] evil. Therefore, do not be foolish and thoughtless, but understand and firmly grasp what the will of the Lord is.**
>
> Father, I consider my life and my relationship with my spouse as sacred and precious. I will not waste a moment of my time but will be a good steward of conducting my day, because someday I will be held accountable to You. In Jesus' name, Amen.

THE FOUNDATIONS OF RECOVERY - PART 2 DIGGING DEEPER

Use the next page for examples to help complete your travel and vacation plan

Practices to maintain

- Dailies with my wife
- Reading of recovery materials
- Prayer (morning and evening)
- Making one call
- Exercise and time alone each day
- Attending regular group check-in (if occurring on that night and not flying)
- Keeping weekly accountability meeting (if occurring on that night and not flying)
- Adhering to 24-hour tell policy if applicable
- Rubber bands for wrist and around remote or any other possible boundary-violating object or place in the hotel room (as a reminder)
- Completing at least 1 page of at least 1 workbook/activity guide a day

Adhering to good sleep (all media off by 8 pm)

Consequences

If any of the above boundaries are violated, an accountability brother and partner must know within 24 hours and new consequences must be applied (written in stages, so that each consequence corresponds with a violation):

1. Twitter profile deleted
2. In-house separation
3. Out of house for 24 hours
4. Turning in smart phone for a pinwheel phone

Boundaries

- No staring at other women on the beach
- Before and after beach calls:
    - Sunday:
    - Monday:
    - Tuesday:
    - Wednesday:
- Side hugs only (on meeting and departure or when appropriate)
- No sexual contact of any kind
- No drinking/dancing/flirting with a woman
- No visits to any hotel room other than my own unless with another person
- No inordinate focus on chivalry (opening doors, paying for meals or physical/trait affirmations. This also includes grooming behaviors such as extensive use of pet names or excessive praise in forms such as putting hearts on text responses or excessively flowery words verbally/sexually)
- No prolonged (deep, embracing and longer than two seconds) chest-to-chest hugs with any women (Unless caught off guard or unavoidable, no chest-to-chest hugs at all).

PARTNER CONNECT Share your recovery travel and vacation plan with your partner.

Life in Recovery

Exercise 51

Many things can change going forward after this exercise book. Many things can stay the same. You will face decisions to either drift away from your partner, away from sexual addiction sobriety, and/or toward a healthy mindset and relationship with your God. It's your choice.

Below you will explore the ways you can choose to stay in recovery and a right relationship with God.

Area of Recovery	How will you stay in Recovery?
Career	
Marriage Status	
Friendships	
Relationships with your Children	
Physical Health & Status of Sexual Diseases	
Feelings about Self	
Feelings about Others	
Spiritual Health	
Hobbies/Interests	
Other:	
Other:	

> **Romans 12:2 AMP** And do not be conformed to this world, but be transformed and progressively changed by the renewing of your mind, so that you may prove what the will of God is, that which is good and acceptable and perfect [in His plan and purpose for you].
>
> Father, only through prayer and scripture will my mind be truly renewed and rewired for success. As I meditate on Your word and discipline my thought life and my actions to conform with Your will, I will see amazing changes in my life. Your plan for me is good. Your plan for me is perfect! I thank You for it! In Jesus' name, Amen.

THE FOUNDATIONS OF RECOVERY - PART 2 DIGGING DEEPER

ALL Step Connection: Calling others in recovery and staying convicted and vulnerable about your actions and daily behaviors has been essential for your recovery. Make a call and share what you have planned for with your **most trusted recovery partner**. This can be your sponsor or someone you have bonded with throughout your time in recovery. Record any meaningful suggestions they had for staying in recovery.

Area of Recovery	How **they** said you stay in Recovery?

Sponsoring Others

Exercise 52

Written by Jeff A. from Washington

You are on a path of recovery that has changed your heart. The life before you entered recovery has given you a story that is worth sharing to help others in their journey. By helping others, you will strengthen your recovery as well. Each time you share your story and encourage another in theirs, you grow.

It is extraordinary to be an individual walking in recovery from sexual addiction or intimacy avoidance. You begin seeing the world differently, and you can share this knowledge through sponsoring others that are not as far along as you.

Because you are at the end of this exercise book (approximately 1 year later) ,your 12-step process should be nearing its end. You have a story to tell through those steps. You have knowledge of what it takes to dig deep into inventory, confess your struggles to others, accept forgiveness for your wrongs, and make amends with those you've harmed. Then, you are attempting to live a life being honest, vulnerable, and reflective in a lifestyle of living out your changed heart.

Choosing to sponsor someone is an honor. Consider someone in your recovery circle that is not as far along as you that is needing a sponsor. Approach them and ask if they would like a sponsor. Refer them to the "choosing a sponsor" exercise earlier in this book. If you both are open to walking in recovery together, commit to it. Set up typical times to talk. Know their sobriety date. Know their story. Use the space below to reflect and set up commitments.

I chose to sponsor _____ and they agreed to have me.

We will typically connect _____times per week on _____(day(s) of week) at _____(time).

Here is my story I would like to share…

I reflected and heard patterns and struggles in their story…

Step 12 Connection: Write a prayer for them, speaking specifically for their areas of struggle, the partnership they want to heal, and for direction on how to approach being their sponsor.

Acts 20:28 Pay careful attention to yourselves and to all the flock, in which the Holy Spirit has made you overseers, to care for the church of God, which he obtained with his own blood.

Father, sponsoring others is a serious responsibility. And I take this responsibility to heart. I know that a day will come when I must report to You what I have done for those under my care. I promise to pay careful attention to all under my guidance. I promise to do the best I can for each one. In Jesus' name, Amen.

Parting Words

In closing, I would like to thank you for using this workbook. We hope that it was helpful to you. While I know the road is long and tough to navigate, I encourage you to keep pressing on. As Winston Churchill once said, "If you are going through hell, keep going." If you do the work, don't give in, and seek help along the way, I know you will find your way out of the painful circumstances in which you have found yourself. We wish you healing, comfort, peace, and wholeness in your recovery journey.

Addendum

Yearly Tracker

Use this tracker combined with the weekly check-in to keep track of your efforts in recovery for the next year

Month	Dr/ N/R	Present in Relationship	Rating of Relationship	# of Calls	Recovery Score /100	Month	Dr/ N/R	Present in Relationship	Rating of Relationship	# of Calls	Recovery Score /100
Jan	/ /	/ 10	/ 10		/ 100	July	/ /	/ 10	/ 10		/ 100
	/ /	/ 10	/ 10		/ 100		/ /	/ 10	/ 10		/ 100
	/ /	/ 10	/ 10		/ 100		/ /	/ 10	/ 10		/ 100
	/ /	/ 10	/ 10		/ 100		/ /	/ 10	/ 10		/ 100
	/ /	/ 10	/ 10		/ 100		/ /	/ 10	/ 10		/ 100
Feb	/ /	/ 10	/ 10		/ 100	Aug	/ /	/ 10	/ 10		/ 100
	/ /	/ 10	/ 10		/ 100		/ /	/ 10	/ 10		/ 100
	/ /	/ 10	/ 10		/ 100		/ /	/ 10	/ 10		/ 100
	/ /	/ 10	/ 10		/ 100		/ /	/ 10	/ 10		/ 100
	/ /	/ 10	/ 10		/ 100		/ /	/ 10	/ 10		/ 100
March	/ /	/ 10	/ 10		/ 100	Sept	/ /	/ 10	/ 10		/ 100
	/ /	/ 10	/ 10		/ 100		/ /	/ 10	/ 10		/ 100
	/ /	/ 10	/ 10		/ 100		/ /	/ 10	/ 10		/ 100
	/ /	/ 10	/ 10		/ 100		/ /	/ 10	/ 10		/ 100
	/ /	/ 10	/ 10		/ 100		/ /	/ 10	/ 10		/ 100
April	/ /	/ 10	/ 10		/ 100	Oct	/ /	/ 10	/ 10		/ 100
	/ /	/ 10	/ 10		/ 100		/ /	/ 10	/ 10		/ 100
	/ /	/ 10	/ 10		/ 100		/ /	/ 10	/ 10		/ 100
	/ /	/ 10	/ 10		/ 100		/ /	/ 10	/ 10		/ 100
	/ /	/ 10	/ 10		/ 100		/ /	/ 10	/ 10		/ 100
May	/ /	/ 10	/ 10		/ 100	Nov	/ /	/ 10	/ 10		/ 100
	/ /	/ 10	/ 10		/ 100		/ /	/ 10	/ 10		/ 100
	/ /	/ 10	/ 10		/ 100		/ /	/ 10	/ 10		/ 100
	/ /	/ 10	/ 10		/ 100		/ /	/ 10	/ 10		/ 100
	/ /	/ 10	/ 10		/ 100		/ /	/ 10	/ 10		/ 100
June	/ /	/ 10	/ 10		/ 100	Dec	/ /	/ 10	/ 10		/ 100
	/ /	/ 10	/ 10		/ 100		/ /	/ 10	/ 10		/ 100
	/ /	/ 10	/ 10		/ 100		/ /	/ 10	/ 10		/ 100
	/ /	/ 10	/ 10		/ 100		/ /	/ 10	/ 10		/ 100
	/ /	/ 10	/ 10		/ 100		/ /	/ 10	/ 10		/ 100

Feeling Wheel

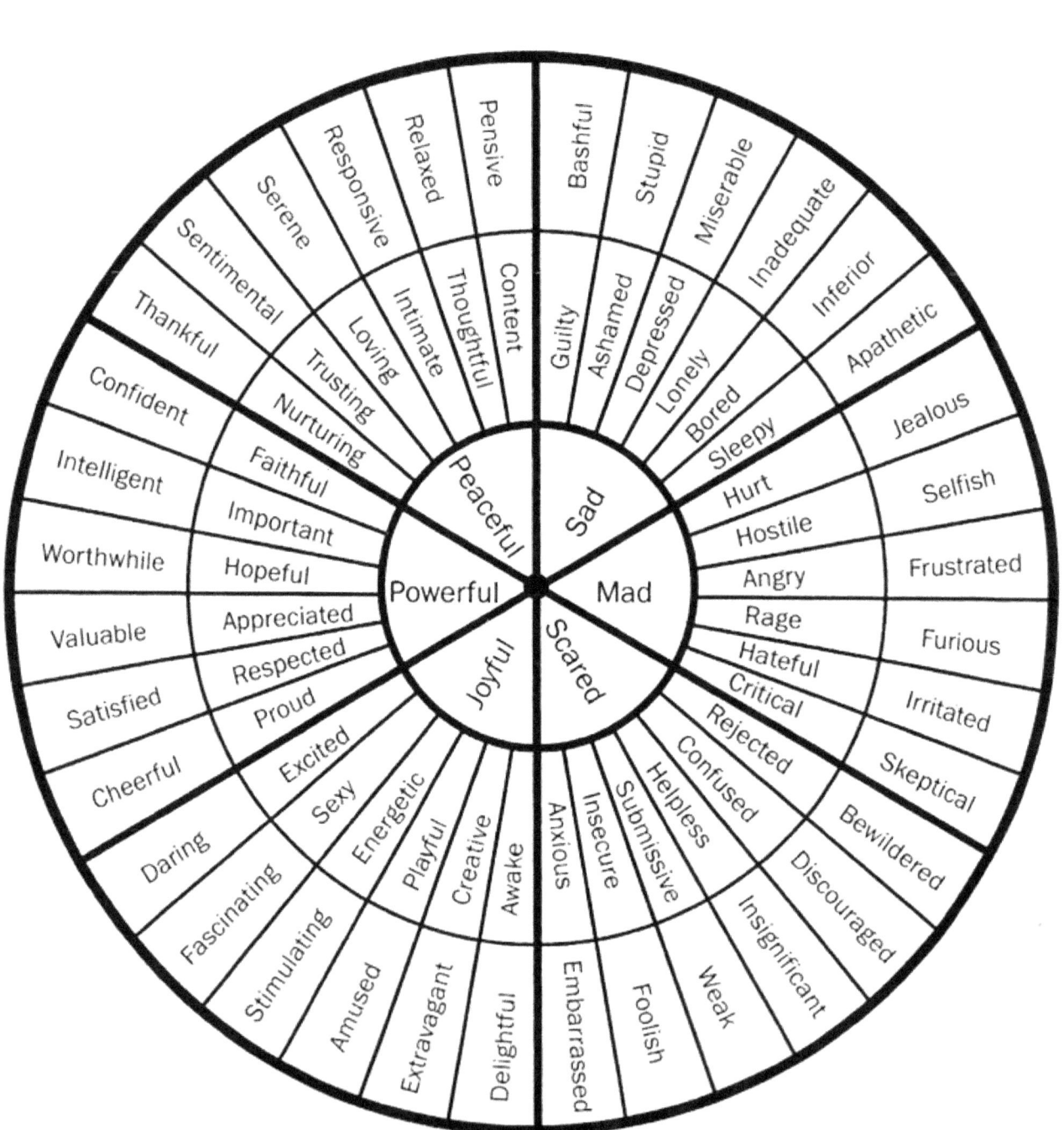

The Twelve Steps for Sexual Addiction

 1 We admitted we were powerless over lust and that our lives had become unmanageable

 2 We came to believe that a power greater than ourselves could restore us to sanity.

 3 We made a decision to turn our will and lives over to the care of our higher power as we understand them.

 4 We made a searching and fearless moral inventory of ourselves.

 5 We admitted to our higher power, to ourselves, and to others the exact nature of our wrongs.

 6 We were entirely ready to have our higher power remove all these defects of character.

 7 We humbly asked our higher power to remove our struggle.

 8 We made a list of all people we had harmed, and we became willing to make amends with them all.

 9 We made direct amends to whomever possible, except when to do so would injure them or others.

 10 We continue to take personal inventory and, when in the wrong, we promptly admit it.

 11 We seek through prayer and meditation to improve contact with our higher power, praying for knowledge of their will for our lives and the strength to carry it out.

 12 Having had a spiritual awakening from our experience through the steps, we seek to share with others and practice our principles in all our relationships.

The Twelve Steps for Intimacy Avoidance

 1 We admitted we were powerless over avoidance and that our lives had become unmanageable

 2 We came to believe that a power greater than ourselves could restore us to sanity.

 3 We made a decision to turn our will and lives over to the care of our higher power as we understand them.

 4 We made a searching and fearless moral inventory of ourselves.

 5 We admitted to our higher power, to ourselves, and to others the exact nature of our wrongs.

 6 We were entirely ready to have our higher power remove all these defects of character.

 7 We humbly asked our higher power to remove our struggle.

 8 We made a list of all people we had harmed, and we became willing to make amends with them all.

 9 We made direct amends to whomever possible, except when to do so would injure them or others.

 10 We continue to take personal inventory and, when in the wrong, we promptly admit it.

 11 We seek through prayer and meditation to improve contact with our higher power, praying for knowledge of their will for our lives and the strength to carry it out.

 12 Having had a spiritual awakening from our experience through the steps, we seek to share with others and practice our principles in all our relationships.

Recovery and 12 Step Prayers

Third Step Prayer (Page 63, AA Big Book)

God, I offer myself to Thee — to build with me and to do with me as Thou wilt. Relieve me of the bondage of self, that I may better do Thy will. Take away my difficulties, that victory over them may bear witness to those I would help of Thy Power, Thy Love, and Thy Way of life. May I do Thy will always!

Fourth Step Prayer (Page 67, AA Big Book)

This is a sick man. How can I be helpful to him? God, save me from being angry. Thy will be done.

Seventh Step Prayer (Page 76, AA Big Book)

My Creator, I am now willing that you should have all of me, good & bad. I pray that you now remove from me every single defect of character that stands in the way of my usefulness to you & my fellows. Grant me strength, as I go from here to do Your bidding. Amen.

Eighth Step Prayer (Page 76, AA Big Book)

Faith without works is dead.

Tenth Step Prayer (Page 85, AA Big Book)

How can I serve Thee? Thy will (not mine) be done.

Eleventh Step Prayer (Twelve Steps and Twelve Traditions, p. 99)

Lord, make me a channel of Thy peace – that where there is hatred, I may bring love – that where there is wrong, I may bring the spirit of forgiveness – that where there is discord, I may bring harmony – that where there is error, I may bring truth--that where there is doubt, I may bring faith--that where there is despair, I may bring hope – that where there are shadows, I may bring light – that where there is sadness, I may bring joy. Lord, grant that I may seek to comfort rather than to be comforted – to understand, than to be understood – to love, than to be loved. For it is by self-forgetting that one finds. It is by forgiving that one is forgiven. It is by dying that one awakens to eternal life. Amen

Serenity Prayer (Reinhold Niebuhr)

God, grant me the serenity to accept the things I cannot change,
The courage to change the things I can,
And the wisdom to know the difference.

40 ways to be IA
(Intimacy Avoidant)

1. **Marked lack of empathy.** Has trouble putting themselves in someone else's shoes. Often comes off as insensitive or uncaring. When others try to share their perspective, they often impose their own views on the situation without listening to the other person's view. Often has trouble understanding cause and effect - in other words, how their actions are contributing to the reactions of others.

2. **Oversensitivity to criticism or perceives criticism when there is none.** This may stem from a fear of rejection, poor self-esteem, or a generally negative view of others' intentions. Oversensitivity to criticism has been linked to negative childhood experiences such as harsh criticism from a parent or caregiver, rejection from peers, or having a parent with unrealistically high expectations. People who are oversensitive to criticism (real or perceived) often have negative cognitive biases that cause them to interpret information in a negative way.

3. **Low emotional expression and bandwidth.** Has an inability or unwillingness (oftentimes both) to express emotion. Emotional range is generally very small (2 or 3 emotions shared, usually some type of anger). The term "emotional bandwidth" refers to someone's ability to handle or engage in emotional stimuli, whether the stimulus is their own or someone else's.

4. **Jumps to conclusions.** Involves jumping to conclusions without having supporting facts. Mind-reading is when people randomly conclude that others are reacting negatively to them. Fortune-telling is assuming things are going to turn out badly and acting like those assumptions are already established facts.

5. **Contempt for self/others.** Contempt for self often comes across as shame and/or self-pity. Contempt for others comes out as grandiosity, belittling, or criticism.

6. **Sabotages emotional connectedness.** According to research studies, people who sabotage their relationships often have low self-esteem, difficulty trusting people (especially their partners), and a fear of commitment or being hurt, abandoned, or rejected.

7. **Reactive vs. Proactive in relationships.** This person appears ambivalent or disinterested in creating opportunities for ongoing, consistent connectedness. Major efforts to show love to their partner only come when the partner is fed up and entertaining the thought of ending the relationship. These efforts often fade away once the partner is reconnected to them, leading to an ongoing cycle that alternates between disinterest, emotional pain, and love-bombing.

8. **Spiritually independent or disengaged.** This person refuses to share any intimate details of their spirituality with their partner, often claiming that their spirituality is "private".

9. **Hoop jumping.** Often a feature of Intimacy Avoidant relationships, the IA will make their partner jump through a series of "hoops" to receive love. Much of this behavior is born out of entitlement. IAs often use this behavior as an excuse to withhold intimacy from their partner or criticize them for a "lack of performance."

10. **Defensiveness.** Defensive people often have issues of power and control. They often perceive confrontation and/or accountability as threats. The purpose of defensiveness is typically to protect a person from feeling hurt or shame. Defensiveness comes in many forms, including blame-shifting, silence, denial, and even self-pity.

11. **Prideful and/or Unteachable.** Typically, a person is masking feelings of low self-esteem and self-worth with pride. Pride is often a byproduct of feelings of inadequacy and vulnerability. Being "unteachable" can stem from pride, jealousy, stress, anxiety, or feelings of inadequacy.

12. **Blame-shifting.** People who blame-shift are often in denial about their level of personal responsibility. They often can't accept the fact that they may be at least partially responsible for a failure or mistake. Another reason for blame-shifting is to make the other person feel guilty or shamed, to silence them.

13. **Offended from victim position.** This takes place when a person decides that their role as victim gives them the right to lash out and/or hurt others. Pia Mellody and Terrence Real call this "retaliation." Intimacy Avoidant people often put themselves in the victim position through blame-shifting, shame, and self-pity. This makes it easier to justify bad behavior.
14. **Suspicious of partner.** There are many reasons IAs are suspicious of their partners. Common reasons include adverse childhood experiences that cause a general lack of trust toward others, depression and anxiety, and negative experiences in past relationships.
15. **Gaslighting.** Gaslighting is defined as psychological manipulation, typically over a prolonged period, that causes the victim to question their thoughts, feelings, memories, and perception of reality. Gaslighting typically involves lying but is not the same as lying. People often lie to escape consequences. Gaslighters lie to intentionally cause someone else to doubt themselves.
16. **Stonewalling/Punishing through anger.** Uses anger or silence to control the conversation. With silence, the partner eventually gives up, which is the intent. Anger is often used to intimidate, and punishing through anger is done purposely to teach the person a lesson and make them think twice about saying anything again. In either case, both are being used to silence someone.
17. **Frequent lying.** For IAs, lying often comes in the form of leaving out important information to avoid unwanted consequences. In some cases, habitual lying can be a sign of a more serious personality disorder.
18. **Avoids taking responsibility for actions.** This can be a result of emotional immaturity, denial, a refusal to be vulnerable, or an avoidance of intense feelings of remorse, guilt, and/or shame. In more serious cases, it can be because the person truly feels that accepting consequences is beneath them or does not have any understanding that their actions have consequences.
19. **Breadcrumbing or Love Bombing.** Breadcrumbing is a form of manipulation in which a person gives another person just enough attention and/or love to string them along. Love bombing often comes in the form of excessive flattery, attention, or gifts being used to lure someone to gain security for themselves.
20. **Emotionally disengaged.** This often stems from a deep fear of being ridiculed or rejected. An emotionally disengaged person may have learned from previous relationships that showing emotions made them vulnerable to negative consequences. Emotional disengagement is often developed in the family of origin when one or both parents failed to communicate their emotions or were uncomfortable with the emotions of others.
21. **Feelings are facts.** A person who treats feelings as facts often experiences emotions so intensely that they feel real. This typically stems from emotional immaturity. It's related to the cognitive distortion of emotional reasoning: "I feel it, so it must be true."
22. **Poor self-reflection.** Otherwise known as a lack of self-awareness. People with poor self-reflection are often intensely afraid of judgement and rejection from others. They keep themselves in a "protective bubble." This "bubble" makes it difficult for them to get in touch with their inner selves.
23. **Self-preoccupation.** This often stems from early childhood experiences of feeling rejected by others. They also could have been brought up to believe that they didn't have to consider the feelings of others. Trauma can also play a role because the person may have learned that they couldn't trust others, and this developed into self-preoccupation. Self-preoccupied people are generally emotionally immature.
24. **Labels themselves and others.** Related to the cognitive distortion of Labeling, which is a form of overgeneralization. It can also be related to perfectionism. For example, instead of being able to accept that they made a mistake, a person might label themselves a "loser." Instead of being understanding about the faults of others, they may label others "losers" or "idiots." Instead

of describing a situation realistically, labeling typically involves using inflammatory terms and language.

25. **Focuses on the faults of others.** Typically used as a defense mechanism in order to avoid feelings of guilt, shame, or inadequacy. It can also stem from entitlement when a person feels everyone else it at fault for them not getting what they want or feel they deserve.

26. **Objectification.** Treats their partner, others, and even themselves as objects. This extends far past sexual objectification or reducing someone to the sum of their body parts. Objectification also shows up as treating someone as if there is no need to be concerned about their experiences and/or feelings, a refusal to honor boundaries, treating people as if they were tools to be used for the IA to achieve their own goals, and treating someone as if they were easily replaced with someone else (a refusal to acknowledge someone's uniqueness).

27. **Poor demeanor.** Acts frequently disgruntled, angry, or irritated. Doesn't listen to their partner's feelings or discounts their experience. When asked to participate in the nurturing of the relationship, acts like it's a huge imposition. When asked to be accountable for past and/or present actions, responds with anger, blame, or pouting.

28. **Sexually disconnected or avoidant.** Doesn't make eye contact during sex or is mentally "checked out." Sex often feels empty and transactional to the partner. Also common is a complete/almost complete avoidance of sex. Couples that have sex 6 or fewer times per year are considered to have a "sexless" relationship.

29. **Sexual gratification outside of committed relationship.** This isn't always the case, but when it is it's typically due to an inability to connect with the partner. For most, this will be done through pornography and masturbation. For some, it will involve getting emotionally or sexually connected with a real person who is not their partner. Sexual addiction and attachment disorders are often underlying issues, especially with serial cheating.

30. **Inability to handle conflict productively.** For some, this will show up as conflict avoidance, stonewalling, and/or people-pleasing. For others, this will involve blame-shifting, denial, and overall defensiveness.

31. **All-or-nothing thinking (black-and-white thinking).** Seeing things in black and white without shades of gray. Tends to associate others and self into 2 categories: good and bad. Signs of all-or-nothing thinking include a tendency to use extreme terms when describing things, perfectionism, inability to see both good and bad in people and/or self, negative self-talk, and fear of trying new things.

32. **An intense need to be right.** Possible reasons for always needing to be right include insecurity, a need for control, a fear of failure, a competitive nature, and cognitive biases or distortions (such as all-or-nothing thinking) that make it difficult to consider alternate perspectives or admit it when wrong.

33. **Easily offended.** Often related to the cognitive distortion of personalization, which is assigning blame to oneself for circumstances out of one's control. Other reasons include unresolved psychological or emotional issues, a perception that their honor or personally held beliefs are being attacked, a generally negative emotional state, or the struggle to consider another's point of view.

34. **Maximization and minimization of faults and/or good deeds.** Tends to see others' faults as "huge" and their own as "not so bad." Tends to see their contributions as "huge" and others' contributions as minimal. In extreme cases, this can be due to grandiosity that contributes to a false sense of self-importance.

35. **Workaholism.** Many workaholics seek approval and become overly focused on work and "busyness" to gain approval and respect from others. Sometimes workaholism also occurs when the person is trying to avoid intimacy in their relationships.

36. **Plays the victim.** Playing the victim is a manipulative tactic. It is often used to avoid taking responsibility, gain sympathy and attention from others, and/or to discredit the experience and feelings of a person they have wronged.

37. **Hero or Zero.** Since IAs tend to see things in black and white without shades of gray, they tend to see themselves as a complete "hero" without faults or a "zero" with nothing but faults. This mentality often leads to blame-shifting, going "victim," and even complete denial of the issues.

38. **I did it my way.** This is an unwillingness to accept influence from their partner. IAs are typically highly independent and often don't listen to the suggestions of their partners when making decisions. Many partners define an IA partner as "an island."

39. **Cynical Script.** A bad story being played repeatedly in the person's head to excuse their poor treatment of the partner. The cynical script is often used to play the victim.

40. **Married but Unloved:** If married, the partner feels as if they are alone in it all. Many partners married to Intimacy Avoidants describe this as a surprise. It is common for Intimacy Avoidants to act differently before marriage than after marriage. Once the commitment to marriage is made, Intimacy Avoidants start to pull away from their partners in the ways that matter most. Partners may describe the relationship as sexless, devoid of intimacy, and disconnected.

Workgroups and Intensives

Men's Becoming Well Workgroups

Some guys have been in groups before; others have not. If you're committed to recovery from Sexual Addiction, Intimacy Avoidance, or Infidelity and are committed to rebuilding trust in your marriage, then our Men's Becoming Well Workgroups will be a good fit for you. Our men's groups focus on building and maintaining integrity, restoring intimacy in relationships, and rebuilding trust. They concentrate on two things: how to stop acting out and be accountable for the behavior that is breaking trust in the relationship, and how to develop the character and empathy it will take to support the relationship moving forward. And unlike many recovery groups out there, our guys are both finding sobriety and maintaining it.

Our groups are led by trained facilitators who have walked through many of these issues themselves, know how to stay sober, and know how to win in their relationship. The groups are small in size (no more than 8 people) so that each person can get the attention they need to address specific issues.

Each week, participants will hear a teaching from a trained professional and receive assignments and exercises that facilitate recovery for both themselves and their relationships. Participants will also have access to an online education portal, videos that explain the concepts talked about during group, and tutorials on how to work exercises and complete assignments.

Another thing that makes our groups different is that we welcome input from the wounded partners. Most programs exclude the partner, expecting that they stay in a relationship and take their partner's word for it that they're doing the work. When we hear from partners about past experiences, they often complain that nothing was shared with them, and they didn't even know what was going on most of the time.

Although we want to stress that the men need to own and work through their own recovery, and no partner can do that for them, we assign exercises to include the partner in rebuilding the relationship. Additionally, we offer a free monthly video conference call in which we update partners on what the guys will be working on that month and allow them to ask questions. Those meetings are typically led by Matt and Laura Burton personally.

Join a Men's Becoming Well workgroup today
www.BecomingWellInstitute.com

Men's Sexual Addiction, Infidelity & Intimacy Avoidance Recovery Intensives

Sexual addiction, infidelity, and intimacy avoidance can be isolating. Whether they're recovering from physical or emotional affairs, infidelity through pornography or other forms of sexual acting out, or intimacy avoidance, men entering recovery often feel like they are going it alone. Maximize your intensive experience by joining with other men to work through issues common to sexual addiction, infidelity, and intimacy avoidance. A Men's 3-Day Recovery Intensive can provide you with a safe environment to voice your pain and concerns, and to learn techniques for healing.

Intensives in a group format provide hope that you are not alone. You will hear the stories and struggles of others. You will also hear from Laura Burton, a trained and certified coach and a partner of someone who struggled with intimacy avoidance and pornography addiction. This will allow you to gain a deeper understanding of what both you and your partner are experiencing during this tough time in your relationship. You will not only see things through your relationship's historical lens, but through the eyes of others. This can help you gain a much-needed perspective that will help you move forward in recovery. Intensives focus on breaking the hold that addiction, infidelity, and intimacy avoidance have had on you and your partner. We partner with you to solve the issues that are holding you back from having the connection you have always wanted.

The Men's 3-Day Recovery Intensive offers daily group meetings and instruction by experts to ensure that the experience is tailored to you. Contact us today to schedule your intensive. Even if you are not currently in a relationship, the perspective you will gain throughout the intensive will help prepare you for the future—however that may look.

- Intensives are limited to 14 men per session.
- They take place at the Becoming Well Institute Intensive Center in sunny Tucson, Arizona.
- This includes an intake and assessment to identify your specific needs.
- We currently offer 2 distinct intensives for men: one with a focus on intimacy avoidance and one with a focus on sexual addiction and sexual/emotional infidelity.
- Each intensive is comprised of a combination of workgroups, group education, homework, exercises to work on with your partner, and personalized recovery plans.
- Contact us for pricing.

Our intensive center is located in beautiful, sunny Tucson, Arizona.

Learn more or sign up for a Men's Recovery Intensive today
www.BecomingWellInstitute.com

Sober Is Not Well
Men's "Going Deeper" Healing Intensives

Are you working on your recovery from porn/sexual addiction and intimacy avoidance? If so, why is your marriage still struggling so much and why do you still have behaviors and/or belief systems that are stunting you and your marriage from truly becoming well?

Why are you still stuck? Why aren't you getting a lot better? Why isn't your marriage getting a lot better? Because Sober is not Well. The areas underlying the SA and IA must be addressed. It's time to take another step in your recovery journey and focus on the roots.

In the Men's "Going Deeper" Healing Intensive, you'll focus on 4 specific areas of the 16 roots that slow or block recovery. These areas will be identified through a 2-part assessment process, one with you and the other getting your partner's input. You will spend your intensive time focused on the 4 identified focus areas in a process we call "Depth Work." That work will happen throughout the 3 ½-day intensive. The 16 root areas of potential intensive focus are:

Past Hurts Focus: Healing the injuries of your past to lessen their impact on you today and in the future.

- o Trauma Focus; o Loss Focus; o Neglect Focus; o Abandonment Focus

Adaptive Behaviors Focus: Dismantling recurring struggles that are destroying you and/or your marriage and have you stuck.

- o Other Addictions/Addiction Swapping Focus; o Anger Focus; o Specific Avoidance Focus; o Sexless Marriage Focus (Relational Sexual Avoidance); o Shame Focus; o Chronic Lying Focus; o Low or Lack of Empathy Focus; o Over Controlling of Self & Others' Focus; o Narcissistic Characteristics Focus; o Perpetual Victim Focus; o Emotional Immaturity Focus; o Chronic Negative Thinking Focus

The Details:

- Men's Healing Intensives are limited to 14 men per week.
- Healing Intensives take place on Thursday-Sunday.
- Your intensive will include intake assessment sessions to identify your particular needs.
- Each intensive weekend is comprised of groups, learning, processing, specific exercises, and personalized recovery plans.
- The time commitment per day is approximately 8 hours.
- Healing Intensive weekends are offered in-person only.

Our intensive center is located in beautiful, sunny Tucson, Arizona.

www.BecomingWellInstitute.com

Couple's Group Intensives
Moving couples from "Shattered to Strong"

Sexual addiction, infidelity, and intimacy avoidance can be isolating. Couples entering recovery often feel like they are going through it alone. Maximize your intensive experience by joining with other couples to work through issues common to infidelity and intimacy avoidance. A Couple's Group Intensive can provide you with a safe environment to voice your pain, concerns, and learn techniques for healing. Often, couples working through infidelity feel alone, judged, and hopeless. Intensives in a group format provide hope that you are not alone. You will hear the stories and struggles of others. This will allow you to gain a deeper understanding of what you and your partner are going through during this crisis. You will not only see things through your relationship's historical lens but also through the eyes of others. This can help you gain a much-needed perspective that will move you forward in recovery.

Group Intensive Weekends offer daily group meetings, instruction by experts, and individual sessions to help ensure that your experience is tailor-made for you. Couples leave feeling validated, understood, and hopeful— even if they were initially nervous about sharing their experience with others. Group Intensive Weekends will allow you to make connections with other people who understand what you are going through. This makes it possible for you to receive ongoing support through the relationships you form over the weekend. Couples will leave the Intensive with three distinct recovery plans: one for the wounding partner, one for the wounded partner, and one for the relationship.

- For couples who are in crisis after the recent discovery or disclosure of infidelity.
- For couples who are stuck and don't know how to get better.
- For couples who have experienced the isolation of infidelity, addiction, and intimacy avoidance and want to join a community of people who understand.
- For couples who want to learn from the experience of others in a safe environment.
- For couples who have done recovery work and want to deepen their experience.
- For couples who need a safe space to deal with what happened without feeling judged.
- For couples who want to hear from experts on how to recover from infidelity.
- For couples who want to accomplish in 3 days what normally takes 4-6 months.

The Details:

- Group Intensives take place in person on Thursday, Friday, and Saturday.
- Group Intensive Weekends include intake and assessment sessions to identify your specific needs.
- Each Group Intensive Weekend is comprised of a combination of workgroups, learning, homework, couple-specific exercises, and personalized recovery plans.
- The time commitment per day for Intensive Weekends is approximately 8-10 hours.

Learn more or sign up for a Couple's Group Intensive today
www.BecomingWellInstitute.com

Couples 7-Day: All In One Group Intensives

Are you a guy or married to a guy who's stuck or in a downward spiral, relationally or in your individual recovery, and who's unable to do what's needed/necessary to heal the shattered trust in your relationship?

What if you could experience all 4 intensives that Becoming Well Institute offers in a week? This means he could get the help he needs for his addiction and/or avoidance, as well as begin to heal the roots that created them. At the same time, she could begin to heal from a broken heart and shattered trust. You, as a couple, could begin to repair what has to date seemed impossible to heal.

Well, you can do all this through our 7-day All-In-One Intensive. At this intensive, the woman does key segments of the Women's Wounded Partner Intensive with other women also attending. The man does key segments of the Men's Recovery Intensive and Men's Going Even Deeper Intensive with the other men. Both partners work through key segments of the Couples Group intensive together, with the focus on helping couples navigate SA and IA recovery and Rebuilding Trust.

The four intensives that this all-in-one draws from:

- The Men's Recovery Intensive is for men striving to find lasting sobriety from porn addiction, sexual addiction, physical infidelity, emotional infidelity, intimacy avoidance, and/or sexual avoidance.
- The Wounded Partners Healing Intensive is for partners impacted by their wounding partner's sexual betrayal, intimacy avoidance, and/or sexual avoidance behaviors.
- The Men's "Going Deeper" Healing Intensives focus on the roots that created the addictive and destructive behaviors.
- The Couples Group Intensive helps couples understand what couple recovery looks like and what it takes to repair and rebuild the relationship, especially in the area of trust. It creates clarity and understanding of whether the wounding partner is serious about recovery and what the wounded partner should expect. It also creates a deeper understanding of what the benchmarks and timelines are for healing, all while supplying the tools and practice necessary to increase the likelihood for success.
- BONUS: Our All-In-One Intensive also teaches you how to help your School-Age and Adult Children Heal from the impacts of SA and IA.

For less than half of the total combined cost of all four intensives, you can experience them all. More importantly, you both benefit from the increased recovery & healing each intensive brings.

This is a great option for anyone wanting to accelerate the healing process, because intensives condense 4-6 months' worth of session work into 7 days.

Learn more or sign up for a Guys Group Intensive today

www.BecomingWellInstitute.com

Private Couple's Intensive

Moving couples from "Shattered to Strong"

Couples that attend Our One-on-One Private Couple's Intensives say it helps them understand and begin or advance the long journey of healing from the immediate and ongoing impacts of porn addiction, sexual addiction, infidelity &/or Intimacy avoidance - for both the Wounding and Wounded partner. We are able to take the time to deep-dive into what's specifically destroying the trust, individually and as a couple, and find the recovery you're desperately trying to either rediscover or discover for the first time.

For many couples, this intensive is their last stop before divorce court or a decision to stay permanent roommates. Couple after couple says that their time at the intensive allowed them to identify and begin the process of healing the hurt and devastation, as well as giving them a new relational system, as their current one just doesn't work for many reasons.

If you choose a Private Couple's Intensive, we will work with you to identify your specific needs to make sure your concerns are fully addressed in a private setting. Our Private Couple's Intensives are 3 days in length and will address both people in the relationship individually as well as the relationship itself.

Like the Guys Group Intensive, our Private Couple's Intensive is a great option for anyone wanting to accelerate the healing process, because intensives take 4-6 months' worth of session work and condense it into 3 days. You will receive an assessment of your unique issues, 7-8 hours per day of instruction, exercises and tools to help you move forward, and a personalized recovery plan for yourself and/or your relationship. We provide you a shame-free environment to address your specific issues.

And, if you choose a Private Couple's Intensive, we want you to know that partners are always treated with respect, compassion, and validation for the pain that their partner's issues have caused them. As a partner, you will never be blamed or asked to take any responsibility for your partner's choices. Also, if desired, we have full disclosure and polygraph services available.

Learn more or sign up for a Private Couple's Intensive today

www.BecomingWellInstitute.com

Books and Courses

Moving Couples from Shattered to Strong

REBUILDING TRUST

A Couple's Guide to Healing After Betrayal

MATT BURTON
LAURA BURTON

www.BecomingWellInstitute.com

Books and Courses

Moving Couples from Shattered to Strong

REBUILDING

FOR CHRISTIANS

A Couple's Guide to Healing After Betrayal

MATT BURTON
LAURA BURTON

www.BecomingWellInstitute.com

Books and Courses

Moving Partners from Shattered to Strong

Mending After Betrayal

BOOK AND WORKBOOK

LAURA BURTON

www.BecomingWellInstitute.com

Books and Courses

Moving Partners from Shattered to Strong

Mending After Betrayal

BOOK AND WORKBOOK FOR CHRISTIANS

LAURA BURTON

www.BecomingWellInstitute.com

Books and Courses

www.BecomingWellInstitute.com

Books and Courses

www.BecomingWellInstitute.com

Books and Courses

Books and Courses

www.BecomingWellInstitute.com

Books and Courses

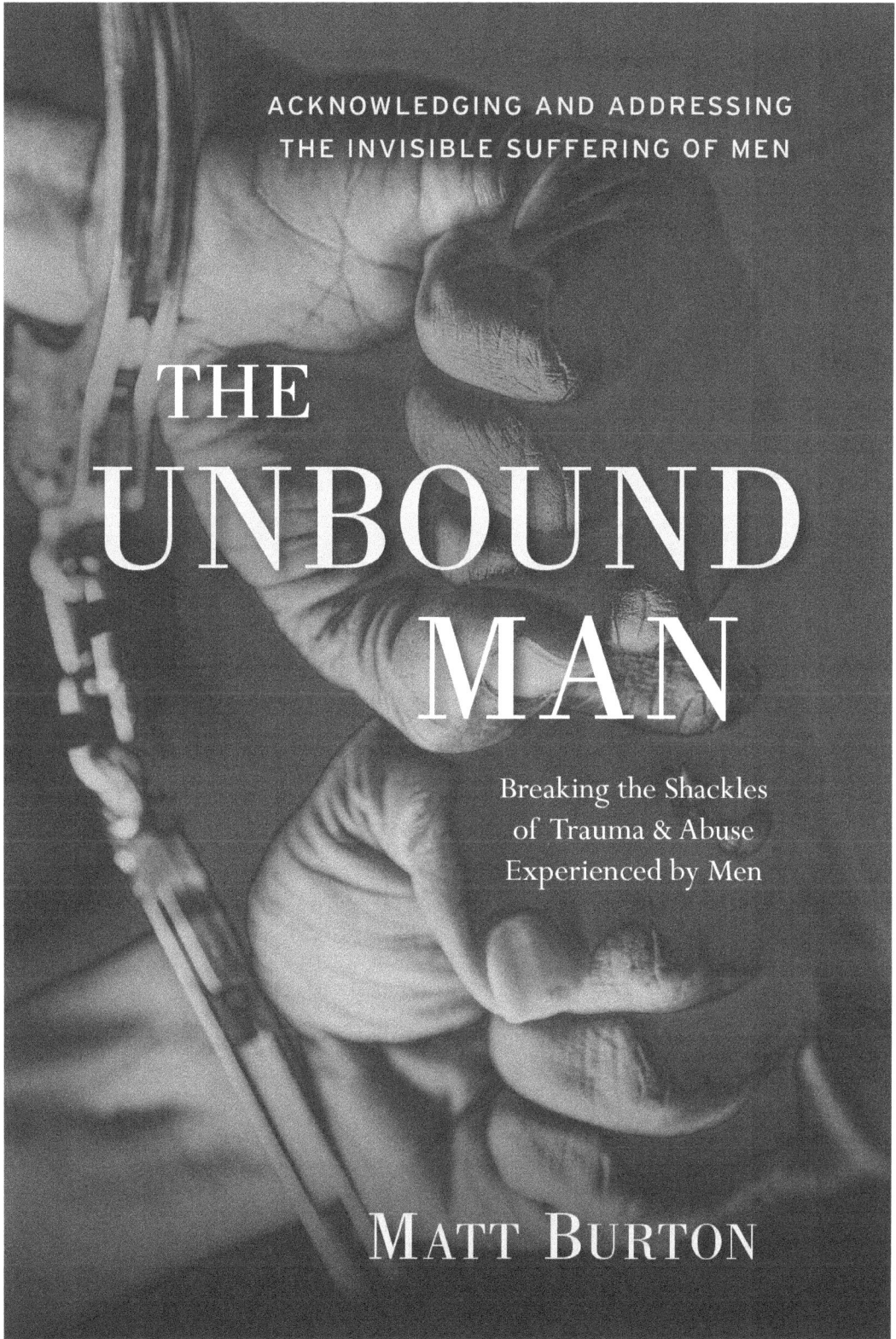

www.BecomingWellInstitute.com

Books and Courses

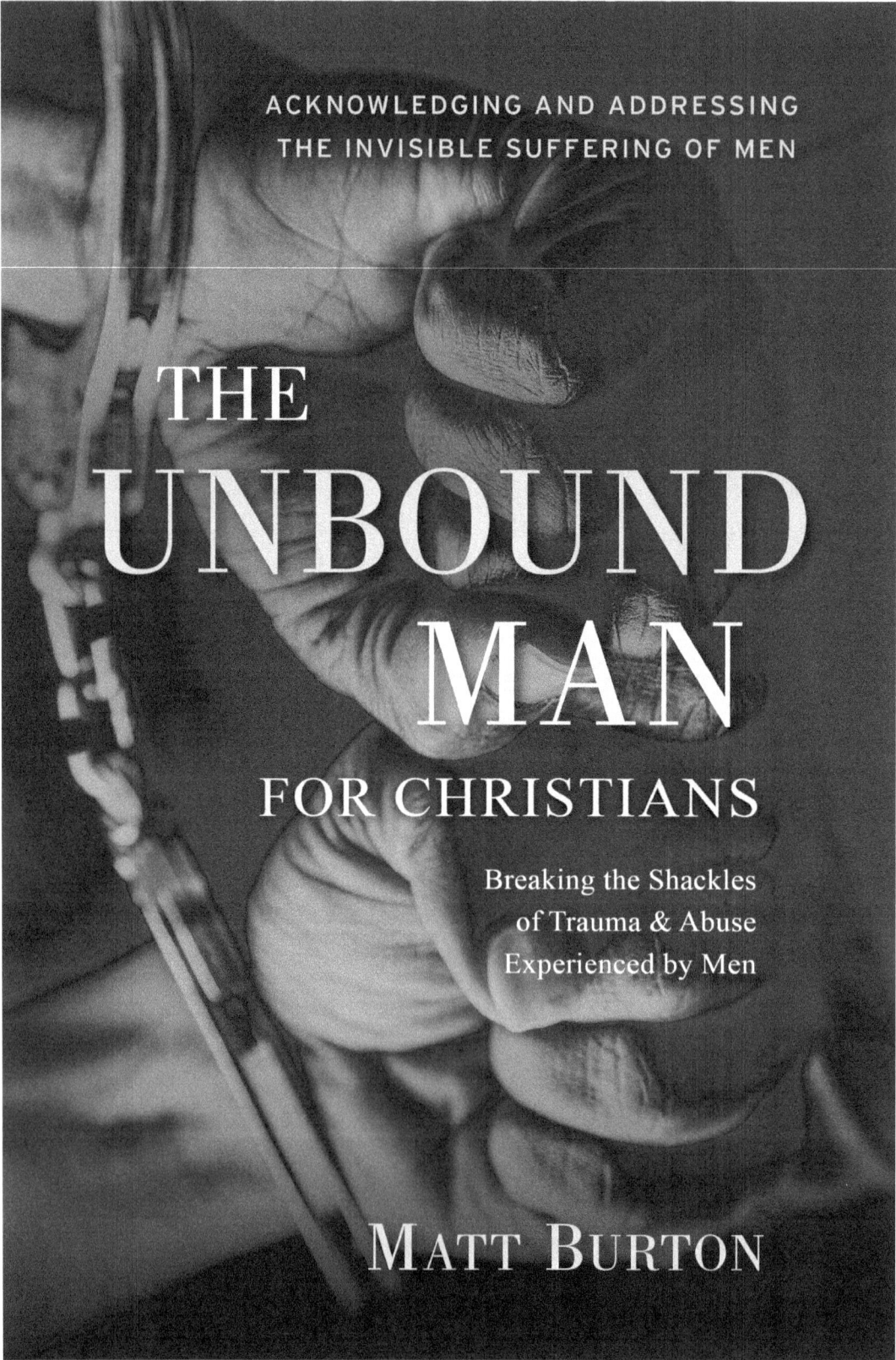

www.BecomingWellInstitute.com

Books and Courses

Books and Courses

Books and Courses

www.BecomingWellInstitute.com

Books and Courses

Part 2
Digging Deeper

Moving from
Shattered to Strong

THE FOUNDATIONS OF RECOVERY

From Sexual Addiction
And Intimacy Avoidance
For Christians

MATT BURTON
KEVIN ROSE
LAURA BURTON

www.BecomingWellInstitute.com

Connect with Us

 www.facebook.com/mybecomingwell

 Becoming Well (@mybecomingwell)

 Becoming Well (@mybecomingwell)

 www.mybecomingwell.com

 info@mybecomingwell.com

 520-355-5322

www.ingramcontent.com/pod-product-compliance
Lightning Source LLC
LaVergne TN
LVHW081457060526
838201LV00057BA/3059